A
LIFE
THAT
MATTERS

Michelle —
Here's to making
a difference!

P.h Dallina

A
LIFE
THAT
MATTERS

Five Steps to Making a Difference

P.K. HALLINAN

Kregel
Publications

ISBN 978-0-8254-4199-8

Library of Congress Cataloging-in-Publication Data

Printed in the United States of America

12 13 14 15 16 / 5 4 3 2 1

For Jeanne

I'm just trying to matter.
—June Carter Cash

CONTENTS

INTRODUCTION

In the room the women come and go
Talking of Michelangelo.
T.S. ELIOT, "THE LOVE SONG OF
J. ALFRED PRUFROCK"

I'd like to be clear right up front: All life matters. I would never say otherwise. What this book is about, however, is having a life that matters to *you*.

In this country, more than half the people in the workforce don't like their jobs.[1] One of the main reasons is that they don't feel fulfilled. If this describes you, I believe my observations and suggestions can help.

Not everyone has the same desire to leave an imprint on the world. For me, however, impact has always been a major issue. By my early twenties, I was already a father with two young sons, and I worked as a toy department manager for a major retailer. It wasn't a bad job, but I remember being overwhelmed by the pointlessness of my life. All I was doing was making money, putting it in the bank, spending it;

making money, putting it in the bank, spending it—
and on and on.

I was bored to death.

One night in bed, with my wife sound asleep beside
me and the rain pelting the roof, I had a real heart-to-
heart talk with myself.

What do you want to do?

What do you want to be?

What would make you feel good about yourself?

I didn't have all the answers, but I knew one thing
for certain: I wanted my life to matter. I wanted to
make a difference in the world around me. I wanted
people to know I had been here. Or, as it is sometimes
poetically put, I wanted to leave a footprint.

When I awoke the next morning, I decided to become a famous novelist. I chose this career because it
sounded like an easy way to make a lot of money—and
also a good way to reach a lot of people. I figured all a
novelist ever did was smoke cigarettes and type. How
hard could it be?

Well, it also helps if you know how to write, but
that didn't stop me. I plowed ahead and churned out
two really terrible manuscripts about a character—
based loosely on myself—who was much smarter and
wittier than every other character in the story. Both
manuscripts are now in a landfill in Kearny Mesa,
California, where they belong.

To a degree, life happens *to* us. That is, we occasionally must react to something that confronts us
suddenly out of nowhere—something we didn't plan,

weren't expecting, and maybe didn't even want. This forces us to do something we might not otherwise ever have done but that significantly changes our lives. That's exactly what happened to me.

Christmas was drawing near. It was early evening, and I was loafing around in the living room, watching television instead of typing away on my third awful novel. My wife came into the room with a big smile on her face and said, "Honey, you're a writer. Why don't you write a little children's book for our kids as a Christmas present?"

I remember liking the fact that she called me a *writer*—I sat up a little taller—but I think she was just being generous. I had never written a children's book, I had barely even read any children's books, and I certainly didn't know how to illustrate a children's book. So I said, "Sure."

This was a life-changing answer.

Over the next two weeks, I scribbled out a little story, drew some pen-and-ink cartoons of my kids, and eventually cranked out a real gem called *Kenny and Mikey Meet the Jungle People!* As ridiculous as this book was, the kids liked it. Much to my surprise, so did everyone else! Family, friends, uninvited guests—everyone said I should write more children's books. So I did.

Forty years have now passed, and I have written and illustrated more than ninety children's books and have sold almost ten million copies worldwide. I feel I have left a footprint. I think "leaving a footprint" is what June Carter Cash had in mind when she would say, "I'm just trying to matter"—reported by many to be one of her favorite responses to questions regarding her personal aspirations.

If there is any one reason why I have sold so many books in my career, it's because I decided very early on only to write books that help children and parents live better and happier lives.

I was walking down the street one day when I saw a dump truck rumbling by. On the side of the truck was this slogan: "Find a Hole and Fill It!" I loved it! I decided right then to do exactly the same thing with my children's books. I would look for the empty spots—the unfulfilled areas—in people's lives and fill them as best I could. This led very quickly to a standard of only writing books that promote good old-fashioned family values.

What I didn't realize at the time was that these traditional, godly values never change. This fact alone has kept many of my books in print for more than twenty-five years. My books never grow old. They never go out of fashion.

Also, as my young readers grow up with my books—as they mature and change—what they get out of the books changes too. For this reason, I originally called my series of children's books "Values for Life." However, by the time I got around to trying to trademark this slogan, it was already taken. So my publisher and I settled on Lifelong Values for Kids. Not quite as clever, but perfectly descriptive of what my books are intended to be.

The real payoff for me has been in how my books

have achieved everything I hoped they would. I remember a woman who approached me several years ago at a book signing at an elementary school. She was clutching one of my books that looked like it had been buried in a coal mine and only recently dug up. She asked if I would mind signing it, even though she wasn't buying it new that day. I happily agreed. She went on to tell me that her son, who had just turned fourteen, was throwing away all his kiddy books, except one. Mine. This was the only children's book he owned that he did not want to part with. I thanked her profusely for sharing that bit of encouragement with me.

It turns out my books have filled a lot of holes in a lot of lives over the years. I feel extremely blessed by this. It helps me feel—to a degree—that my life really does matter.

After forty years of observing life and filling holes, I want to share with you what I consider to be the five most important steps you can take if you want to feel that you have done something valuable with your life:

1. Work hard.
2. Go in the strength you have.
3. Finish what you start.
4. Be patient.
5. Help other people along the way.

These five steps to making a difference are tried-and-true principles that will work for anyone.

I know they will work for you.

WORK HARD

If I'm a genius, why do I have to work so hard?
THEODORE "DR. SEUSS" GEISEL

Work hard. This probably sounds like a no-brainer. And it is. There is simply no substitute for hard work.

Years ago, at an awards dinner, Random House president Bennett Cerf was introducing Dr. Seuss (Ted Geisel) at the podium and preparing to hand him an award. In his remarks, Cerf said, "On our whole publishing list [which included William Faulkner, Truman Capote, John O'Hara, James Michener, Sinclair Lewis, Moss Hart, James Joyce, Gertrude Stein, and Irwin Shaw], Dr. Seuss is our only true genius." That's when Dr. Seuss responded, "If I'm a genius, why do I have to work so hard?"

As an aside, I got to meet Dr. Seuss about thirty years ago at a book-launching party for a mutual friend of ours, Spencer Johnson, author of such mega-hits as *The One-Minute Manager* and *Who Moved My Cheese?* I had met Spencer several years earlier, due to our shared interest in writing children's books. I was working on my seventh children's book, and Spencer was working on a whole slew of children's books called Value Tales. When I sent a proposal to the University of California at San Diego for a class I wanted to offer, called Writing Picture Books for Children, they informed me they already had a children's author on staff. They added, though, that if this other author was willing to let me teach a second, similar class, that they would be fine with it. That's how I came to meet Spencer. We quickly became friends, and I even ended up ghostwriting one of his Value Tales, a book called *The Value of Courage: The Jackie Robinson Story.*

Anyway, this was now several years later, and Spencer had already written *The One-Minute Manager* and was launching his newest work, *The Precious Present.* The party was held in someone's beautiful home, located in the hills above La Jolla Cove, near San Diego, with a gorgeous view of the Pacific Ocean. I lived in a tiny, two-bedroom apartment in Pacific Beach, about ten miles south of La Jolla, and I felt honored to have been asked to attend.

When I walked into the living room, I was amazed to find how packed the place was. There were at least fifty people in the room, and the noise level was already at a roar. I eased in, took a glass of punch from the punch bowl, and looked around to see if I knew anyone. I spotted Spencer first. He was near the back of the room, holding court, smiling and laughing with a group of his admirers, and wearing what looked like a set of loose-fitting white pajamas. I thought of Hugh Hefner.

Then I spotted a tall, mustachioed, well-dressed individual, holding court in almost the exact center of the room. It was "Dr. Seuss," Ted Geisel, and he seemed to be having a great time.

Although I tend to be shy in these types of situations—something very few of my acquaintances suspect about me—I decided I would never forgive myself if I didn't walk over and introduce myself. So I took a deep breath and weaved my way through the crowd until I was directly in front of him.

"Hello, Mr. Geisel," I said. "My name is P.K. Hallinan. I'm a children's author too!"

(As I have traveled around the country, visiting elementary schools, whenever I tell this story to the kids, I always say that Dr. Seuss cupped his ears—as if he could not hear me above the din—and shouted, "You work in a *zoo*?" This is not really what he said, but it gets a huge laugh from kids and teachers alike. And I love to see everybody go haywire. What he *did* say was, "Huh-h-h?" In other words, he could not hear me.)

As I found myself standing in front of Random House's only true genius, reviewing my options as quickly as I could, I came to the conclusion that shouting at the top of my lungs, "I'm a children's author too!" was just too plebeian. Instead, I smiled sheepishly, nodded, and left.

Since then, I have often laughed to myself about the irony of trying to be boastful to others. I always can count on the room being too noisy—or the person too deaf—to hear my self-aggrandizing proclamation.

God plans it this way.

THE WORKING GENIUS

"If I'm a genius, why do I have to work so hard?" is a great question. But it has an easy answer. Everyone who is successful works hard. *Everyone.* By all accounts, football great Jerry Rice—the All-Pro wide receiver for the San Francisco 49ers and arguably the best to ever play that position—was also one of the NFL's hardest workers. He consistently showed up for practice earlier, and went home later, than any of his teammates. That kind of work ethic moves mountains.

In my own career, I have learned the "genius" of hard work for myself. A lot of people say, "I bet being a children's author is a lot of fun." It isn't. It's extremely rewarding, but it isn't "fun" at all. Here's why: Like a lot of other people in the public eye, I often feel like a complete fake. I feel like I'm not *really* a writer. I feel like I'm not *really* an artist. I feel certain that someone is going to come along someday and expose me for the fraud I *really* am. So I strive and strain in order to conceal the evidence. Being a fake is exhausting.

When I first began writing children's books, I had no idea how to draw. I never had studied art of any kind, so I just drew what I could and hoped for the best. One day I got a letter from a publisher, telling me that they wanted to publish a little book I had submitted to them, titled *How Really Great to Walk This Way!* There was only one hitch. They wanted a "real" artist to do the drawings.

So I mulled it over for about one millisecond and said, "Sure." I was okay with their stipulation. In fact, I was so ecstatic about getting accepted for publication that I really didn't care what they did. All I could think was, *Watch out, New York! Here I come!* But when the book finally arrived, my heart sank. I was at work in an underground bunker in Burbank, California, when my phone rang. It was my wife.

"Your book arrived."

"How does it look?"

"Maybe you'd better come home and see for yourself."

This didn't sound good, so I told my boss I felt sick and went home. When I got there, I really *did* feel sick.

It turned out that the publisher's "real" artist hadn't quite fathomed the heart of the book, and his drawings were flat and lifeless—very much like the cartoons in an arithmetic book. I tell people that the reason his art was so flat was because the publisher had paid him a "flat fee" to do the work. It's a great pun, but there's actually some truth to it. We both were paid flat fees because the publisher did not want to pay us royalties and had offered us "work for hire" contracts instead. I was too stupid to know the difference. I was paid a flat fee of $500, and the artist was paid $700. To be honest, though, I didn't much care. I believed it was a first step into something much larger, which would come with time (and it did). My greater concern was the "real" artist's art. It was awful.

I promptly made a deal with myself: I vowed I would never again allow someone else to do the drawings for one of my books.

Which meant that I had to learn how to draw.

About two months later, I started on my next book, a book intended specifically to get kids away from the television and into the great outdoors. I titled it *The Looking Book,* based on the idea that there is so much to see when we really start looking. When it came time for me to do the illustrations, I decided I would do everything I could to make my art acceptable to my publisher. So I poured myself into my drawings like never before. I challenged everything. If I didn't think it was the best work I could do, I did it again.

When all the art was finally done, I made a sickening observation. I had improved so much in the course of illustrating the book that the entire first half was not nearly as well done as the second half. So I had a decision to make: Do I send the manuscript in as-is, or do I reillustrate the first half, hoping that I don't keep improving so much that I have to redraw the second half, too? And then, what if the second half is once again better than the first half, and . . . well, you get the idea.

That's when I made a second deal with myself: If I didn't turn in the best work I was capable of doing, I didn't deserve to be successful. And that settled it. I went back to work and redrew the first half of the book.

Fortunately, I didn't improve enough to warrant redrawing the second half, too.

Then I sent it in.

I am happy to report they published my book, with my art, and started me on my way as both author and illustrator of my children's books. This has made all the difference. While most author/artist combos last for only a couple of years—or a couple of books—I have stayed with my artist for more than forty years now. In fact, I can't get rid of him: I go to sleep with him every night and wake up with him every morning. But this is what has enabled me to create so many published works. One of the principles this turn of events has taught me is that the other side of disaster is always opportunity. Let me say it again: *The other side of disaster is always opportunity.* When I saw the finished product—the flat art—of my first book, I got so upset that I felt like quitting. But as it turned out, if that book had not been so poorly drawn, I would never have had the gumption, or the energy, to become my own illustrator. So, in that sense, something that truly grieved me at the time slowly metamorphosed into one of the best things that ever happened to me. Every setback works this way if we simply turn it over and look at the other side. There's always an unexpected opportunity waiting there.

Another principle I took away from that experience is one I share with schoolchildren all over America: if they're willing to work hard enough, and persistently enough, there is absolutely nothing in the world that can stop them from achieving their goals and reaching their dreams.

I am not a natural artist. But I've found that if I am willing to sit there long enough, drawing and erasing, drawing and erasing, drawing and erasing . . . sooner or later, something *useable* will surface. It's almost like magic. Suddenly, there it is, under all those heaps of eraser gunk, a marketable and semiprofessional drawing. Occasionally, it's a *really good* drawing.

I share this with the kids because, in every school, there are always some students who are just naturally better at things than everyone else. But my example of how hard work can overcome a lack of skill, a lack of talent, a lack of natural ability—or whatever—reaches them. I can see them nodding all over the room.

That being said, nothing can stop *you*, either.

THE ROAD LESS TRAVELED

Dare to dream. It's free and it's often productive. A man named Otto W. Dieffenbach was frustrated by the way his mustache always got covered with ice cream when he was trying to enjoy a milkshake. So one day, he took a cellophane wrapper from a pack of cigarettes, rolled it up, and used it to sip away at his favorite treat. Shortly thereafter, Dieffenbach invented a means for mass-producing cellophane drinking straws.

Another man, King C. Gillette, had been trying to dream up a kind of throwaway product ever since having a conversation with the inventor of the bottle cap.

One morning, when he was shaving with his straight razor, he became angry at how dull the blade was. Very shortly thereafter, he invented the disposable razor blade. There was also Ole Evinrude, who simply got angry one day when the ice cream in his rowboat melted before he could get to his favorite island picnic spot. That's the day Old Ole went home and invented the outboard motor.

Not all dreams are about clever inventions. At some point in our lives, most of us need to ask ourselves, "Am I satisfied with what I've accomplished and where I'm going?" If the answer to this question is no, then the next question should be, "What do I really want to do with my life?"

This is where true dreaming begins.

One of the most important things you can do for yourself is take a personal retreat—or a retreat with your spouse—and dream. Go on a vacation. Take a long walk in the woods. Visit a cabin in the mountains. Escape to a warm, sunny beach—whatever. What matters most is that you set aside some time strictly for you. Then, actively begin considering what kinds of things make you happy. Consider what kinds of things you like to do. And don't limit yourself to the practical or reasonable. Put every dream on the table, no matter how silly or far-fetched. These are *your* dreams, and all of them are possible, no matter how big or small they may seem.

It's been reported that millionaire Malcolm Forbes once said, "The key to success is to enjoy your work.

If you enjoy your work, you are bound to do it well. But more important, if you enjoy your work, you are already successful." I agree. What I appreciate most about this quote is that it truly hits the nail on the head. Having "a life that matters" is not necessarily about finding financial success. It's primarily about self-realization. It's about unleashing the essential you, so that you can live the life you want to live—*whatever* that means to you personally. Frankly, you owe this to yourself. You have one life, and this is your time in the sun. Use it well.

One of the reasons I suggest you take your spouse along on your personal retreat is that he or she probably knows you better than you know yourself. This means you can count on your spouse to rein you in when you're thinking *way* outside your general abilities or usual interests. Bouncing your ideas off an old trusted friend can also be useful, especially if your friend is painfully honest. Candid feedback is always useful. But in the final analysis, the dream is yours—and so is the decision. One of the richest men in the world once said, "I can't give you the formula for success, but I can give you the formula for failure: Try to please everyone."

This brings up an important point: Having "a life that matters" is not just about, or even primarily about, changing careers. Having a life that matters is about emerging from whatever it is that has been holding you back from doing what you were born to do. In many instances, it may mean only readapting yourself to your present environment and finally applying the "essential you" to the tasks you've done a thousand times before—but now with a completely revitalized and more positive approach. (We'll go into greater depth about this in Step Three.) In the meantime, go ahead and dare to dream.

I also encourage prayer. There is nothing quite as helpful as asking the One who created you for His input on what you should be doing with your life. He may surprise you. He may think more highly of your abilities than you do. And He may lead you in a direction that at first seems implausible. That's okay. God always knows what He's doing.

In any case, no matter what you decide to do, don't be afraid to follow the example of poet Robert Frost, who penned these famous lines in "The Road Not Taken": I took the one less traveled by, / And that has made all the difference.

A Step of Faith

> As soon as the priests who carry the ark of
> the LORD . . . set foot in the Jordan, its wa-
> ters flowing downstream will be cut off and
> stand up in a heap. (Joshua 3:13)

As an ordained minister and pastor of a small church, I have used the above Scripture on numerous occasions to illustrate the need to "take the plunge."

Here's the picture: After forty long years of wandering in the desert, the Israelites are finally on the

brink of reaching the Promised Land. It is interesting
to note that, at one mile per day, traveling five days a
week, these people could have walked from Egypt to
China in the same amount of time. So, clearly, they
have been walking in slow, wide circles. Just like a
lot of us. But for them, the journey was almost over.
They were now only a few hundred yards from their
goal. There was just one problem: the Jordan River.
This churning, tumbling, torrent first needed to be
crossed.

This is typical. There is always a Jordan River between us and our goals. As Gilda Radner of *Saturday
Night Live* used to say, "It's always something!" And
she was right. For the Israelites, it was the Jordan. For
you and me, it could be just about anything. But this
much is certain: There is always an element of fear,
danger, and uncertainty involved in attempting to go
forward. So what do we do? Well, here's the gist of
what God told the Israelites to do: *Just do it! Put your
feet in the water, and trust Me to do the rest!*

So, boldly, but certainly nervously, all 2.5 million
Israelites took a big gulp of air and started marching
forward into the Jordan. Here's what happened: As
soon as the soles of the priests' feet touched the water, the water not only stopped, but it was pulled back
almost twenty miles upstream and piled up like blan-
kets near the city of Adam. So, what was God's message to the Israelites—and to us? He won't stop the
river until we put our feet in the water. In other words,
all new endeavors require a step of faith on our part.

GETTING READY TO GET READY

Pioneer Davy Crockett left this advice for posterity: "Be always sure you're right—then go ahead!"[2] In all deference to my childhood hero, he could not have been more wrong. If we wait until we are *sure* we're right, we will never go ahead. There is simply no way of knowing, *for sure*, that we are right, until we move forward and find out.

We have all known people who spent years "getting ready to get ready." But the truth of the matter is that no one is ever completely ready. No one ever has all their ducks lined up. People who wait for this kind of assurance—for this kind of confidence—end up frozen in their tracks. As Professor Harold Hill in *The Music Man* so wisely puts it: "Oh, my dear little librarian. You pile up enough tomorrows, and you'll find you are left with nothing but a lot of empty yesterdays." Amen, Professor Hill.

In my life, I have noticed that there are essentially two types of people when it comes to careers: *Wishers* and *Doers*. Wishers take every class they can find in their field of endeavor, but don't ever actually apply any of it. Doers never take any classes; they go out and make amazing things happen, and then they create new classes for the Wishers to take. This is a simplification, of course, but there is a lot of truth in it. One friend of mine has been writing a novel for the past ten years. She has attended every writing seminar and every writing workshop she can possibly find (including mine), and yet she's still scratching away on chapter 1 today. This is identical to the "professional students" who never stop preparing for their careers, because in their hearts, they don't ever really want to start.

Another way of "getting ready to get ready" is to go out and buy every product you can think of that might help you be more prepared for your new field of endeavor—like buying ten thousand different colored beads for that maybe-soon-to-open crafts store. To a degree, we all do this. When I first became a freelance writer, I spent hours every morning cleaning the house—something I never did before I became a writer—and every other chore I could think of to avoid sitting down at the typewriter. The painful truth about this behavior, though, is that no matter how we try to disguise it, we are really just stalling.

WAITING FOR INSPIRATION

Another—perhaps slyer—form of doing nothing is called "waiting for inspiration." This is very popular among artists of all genres. But it's a bad idea. In fact, when I originally heard the title of the movie *The Crazies*, this is what I thought it was about. I believe that anyone who is "waiting for inspiration" is waiting for a train that has already derailed. It's not coming. Pick up your bags and go home.

One of the real problems about waiting for inspiration is that it assumes the great rush of adrenaline that comes with a good idea will somehow sustain you throughout the project. It won't. For writers, the surge lasts about four pages—then you have the next three hundred pages or so to do on your own. Another problem with waiting for inspiration is that it doesn't pay the bills. Every time I have waited for inspiration, I have ended up falling asleep. Here's how the Bible describes this condition: "A little sleep, a little slumber, a little folding of the hands to rest—and poverty will come on you like a thief and scarcity like an armed man" (Proverbs 6:10–11).

Though inspiration can come on its own, almost any professional will tell you that, more often than not, it has to be *forced* into existence. I call this forcing of creativity "Breaking the Wall."

BREAKING THE WALL

In my life, there are two main reasons why I put things off: *fear* and *loathing*. I fear the unknown and loathe the known. Let me explain: Most of us are intimidated by things we have never done before. This can include something as mundane as trying a different gas station, or something more substantial, like running with the bulls in Pamplona. In my writing business, my reluctance to start a new project is usually caused by a fear I have that when I reach for that great idea, this time it won't be there. Since I never really know where my ideas come from anyway, I'm always a little concerned that maybe my personal "well" has finally gone dry. My other reluctance to start a new project comes from my general loathing of the process. I know what I am getting into. I know how hard the task is going to be. I know how crazy it is going to make me, and my wife, and my dog, Betty, and my cat, Kitty. Someone once said that the reason people who *think* for a living tend to make more money than people who do manual labor is because thinking is so much harder. Though I'm certain that being a coal miner or a steelworker is much harder work than sitting at the computer, I do believe there is some truth to this statement. Ask anyone if they have ever read the entire agreement that came with their credit card. They haven't. Thinking that hard is simply not worth it. It's easier just to cancel your credit card when you finally find out what you've gotten yourself into. This dread of thinking—because it is so hard—is also why students invariably wait until the last minute to cram for a final exam or to write a term paper. No one wants to think hard until they absolutely have to. I would also guess that this *fear* of the unknown coupled with the *loathing* of the known (the process) is what most often accounts for the phenomenon known as "writer's block." I am happy to say I have not experienced this, but only because I have never had the luxury. For as long as I can remember, I have needed to eat.

So, what do we do? How do we stop "getting ready to get ready" and get down to business? How do we overcome the fear and loathing? Here's how: We just turn Mother's picture to the wall, roll up our sleeves, and go to work. Period. There is no other way. The ancient Chinese philosopher Lao Tzu put it like this: "A

thousand-mile journey began with a foot put down."[3]
Like the Israelites on the banks of the Jordan River,
we may need to stop dragging our sandals and step
into the water.

My way of forcing creativity is to sit down with a
pen and a piece of paper and start "wringing out my
brain" until a drop of an idea falls on the paper below.
Sometimes I doodle. Sometimes I scribble. Sometimes
I carefully pen words that are on my mind or in my
heart. But *always*, at some point, a tiny drop of an idea
lands on the paper in front of me. Sometimes it's just
the germ of a concept, but other times it's a *gem* of a
concept!

With any new endeavor, of course, there is always a
start-up period, which can be slow and laborious. In
my career, I call this getting-up-to-speed time "The
"rusty lawn mower effect." It works like this: As a children's author and illustrator, I work from project to
project. This means I often go for months between
books. What happens during these times is that I
get artistically "rusty." Whenever I begin a new work,
then, I invariably go through a period of not being
very good at what I'm doing. I liken this to starting
a rusty lawn mower that has been in the storage shed
all winter. I pull the rope and nothing happens. I pull
it again, and the engine goes *ka-chug!* I pull it a third
time, and it begins to spark and sputter. Finally, my
mental lawn mower will start to hum, and then we're
on our way. Over the years, I have taught myself to
accelerate this relearning time—especially with my

artwork—by challenging myself at the beginning of each project. I try to make the first drawing in my book as detailed and complicated as I possibly can, thereby pushing myself into a higher skill level than if I just do something easy. The result is that I always get my lawn mower up and running more rapidly, and the whole book turns out significantly better.

WHAT YOU CAN EXPECT

When skill and love work together, expect a masterpiece. —John Ruskin

Thomas Jefferson once said, "I'm a great believer in luck, and I find the harder I work, the more I have of it." He was right on the mark. Nothing of value comes easily. Nothing of worth ever comes without a considerable amount of hard work. Change and growth always take time. But that doesn't mean you won't have a wonderful time reaching for the stars. A close friend of mine—who has made himself a millionaire twice over—once said, "There are three things a person needs in order to be happy: someone to love, something to do, and something to look forward to." Of the three, I believe "something to look forward to" is the most important. We all need a reason to get out of bed in the morning. We all need to feel as if our lives have a purpose beyond just surviving day to day. As you read through this book, I hope you will begin to look at yourself, and the world around you, in a whole new way. And I hope you will happily claim the following promise for yourself from a God who deeply loves you: "'I know the plans I have for you,' declares the LORD, 'plans to prosper you and not to harm you, plans to give you hope and a future'" (Jeremiah 29:11).

With your skill and God's love—and some good old-fashioned hard work—you can expect a masterpiece.

Finally, with regard to hard work being the foundational first step toward making a difference, I believe that singer and actress Bette Midler summed it up perfectly when she told an interviewer—regarding how *fleeting* fame can be—that she was not particularly worried about it. "If I lost it all tomorrow," she said, "I would be okay, because I know how I got here." This is a profound truth. Though there are some rare "overnight successes," most of them burn out quickly and never recover. The reason? They don't know how they got there.

Building a dream one step at a time, using the bricks and mortar of hard work, can make virtually anyone a solid success.

Happy building!

STEP ONE:
WORK HARD

GO IN THE STRENGTH
YOU HAVE

Go in this thy might.
JUDGES 6:14 KJV

Every person has at least one special gift, something they are naturally good at. These gifts can be as varied as the stars in the sky. Some people are good athletes. Some people are good with numbers. Some people are good cooks, or good musicians, or good artists. Still others have a flair for science, law, politics, construction . . . whatever.

What's unfortunate is that so many people find themselves in careers that have nothing to do with their primary gift. They are just banging out their days like robots on an assembly line slamming hoods onto automobile chassis. Their work is dull, repetitious, and routine—asking nothing of them—and causing them to feel chronic dissatisfaction with their lives.

It starts early, too. I often ask young college-age people—who are working as baristas, valets, or some such occupation—what they really want to do with their lives. Some will answer, with disarming honesty, "I don't know." Others will light up and share some wonderful dream they have for their future. I always encourage them to go for it. But they rarely do. Two years go by, and they are still making lattes, parking cars, and talking about their "dreams."

What's sad is *not* that they are baristas, valets, waiters, cashiers, or any other type of needed service provider—these are fine jobs. The problem is that so many of these people know they are not doing what they were created to do. I also run into a lot of college students who are experiencing great difficulty trying to decide what they want their major—their primary source of study—to be. Since they have not decided what they want to do with their lives, they cannot decide what they should study. I always recommend that, if they really cannot decide on a major, they choose business as their field of study. Why? Because, sooner or later, everyone finds out that life *itself* is a business. Balancing a bank account is a business. Running a home is a business. Managing one's possessions is a business. Filing taxes is a business. No one can get around it, by it, or away from it. Having a good sense of how business works is an excellent base on which to build any career.

So is identifying—and using—our God-given gifts.

MIGHTY MAN OF VALOR

In the Bible, in the book of Judges, we read that the Midianites routinely raided the land of Canaan to plunder the Israelites' crops. Each harvest, they would descend upon the hapless Hebrews in such great numbers that the Israelites compared them to swarms of locusts. Scripture tells us the Midianites' swift and powerful camels were too numerous to count. The result of this plundering and foraging was near-starvation for the Israelites. So, one day, the Lord decided to put a stop to it.

God appeared, as the Angel of the Lord, to a young man named Gideon, who was threshing wheat in an enclosed winepress, in order to hide his activity from the Midianites. The whole point of threshing wheat is to throw it up in the air so the *wind* can separate the wheat from the chaff. That wasn't happening inside the winepress.

God greets Gideon with these words: "The LORD is with you, mighty warrior" (Judges 6:12). Honestly, if it weren't the Lord Himself saying these words, this greeting would seem like a sarcastic barb. *Mighty warrior?* Gideon was hiding in a winepress! But God always sees beyond our self-imposed limitations, all the way to our full potential. In other words, He already knew more about Gideon's inner strength and abilities than Gideon himself knew.

Like so many men and women called by God, Gideon at first responds with a barrage of doubts and questions. He takes God to task and asks, "If You're so great, how come all this bad stuff is happening to us?"

The Angel of the Lord ignores this question and says, "Go in the strength you have and save Israel out of Midian's hand. Am I not sending you?" (v. 14).

But Gideon falters again and asks, "How can I save Israel? My clan is the weakest in Manasseh, and I am the least in my family" (v. 15).

The Angel responds, "I will be with you, and you will strike down all the Midianites, leaving none alive" (v. 16).

So Gideon obeys. But not right away. First, he needs some reassurance that God is really who He says He is and that He really wants Gideon to take on this overwhelming assignment. So Gideon puts out a fleece and asks God to prove Himself by using the morning dew to wet the fleece, yet keep all the ground surrounding the fleece dry. God complies, but Gideon is still unconvinced; next, he asks God to reverse the process and wet only the ground, but keep the fleece dry. God, now demonstrating the patience of His servant Job, again complies.

At this point, Gideon goes forward, but he still does not fully comprehend the "strength" God has given him. Somehow he amasses an army of 32,000 men (which is quickly winnowed down to 10,000), but God tells him to reduce this number to only 300 men—most likely the oldest and the weakest of the bunch.

Gideon goes into battle with his 300 old-timers

against 125,000 Midianites—and their throng of angry camels—and completely vanquishes them.

You could be another Gideon.

Perhaps you have a recurring ache inside because
you believe there is something "bigger" you are supposed to be doing with your life. But instead of doing
it, you're hiding in a lesser job, threshing wheat in a
windless winepress. Listen for God's voice. He may be
calling you to greater things. He may be asking you
to fully employ the strength He has given you. You
may even have sensed His call on your life, but feel
underequipped and ill-prepared to move forward. So
did Gideon. But God never makes mistakes, and He
never creates failures. He already sees you as a *mighty
warrior*, and He won't be offended if you first put out
a fleece or two. But this much is certain: With your
strength and His guidance, there is no limit to the
odds you can overcome. After all, is *God* not sending
you?

GOING FOR THE GOLD

Back in the 1960s, Peggy Fleming was, without a
doubt, the most graceful, most elegant figure skater
I had ever seen. I distinctly remember watching her
during the 1968 Winter Olympics in Grenoble, France,
as she competed in the "compulsory figures," an element of the figure-skating finals requiring the greatest of physical discipline and precision—and one
I'm not sure they even do anymore. She performed
a series of figure eights, with her long, slender arms

extended like a ballerina's as she glided silently and magnificently in perfect arcs on the manicured ice of the sparsely filled Olympic stadium. She took my breath away. As I watched her, I thought to myself, *This woman owns this sport!* And she did. No one really came close to matching her style and skill, and she handily won the Olympic gold medal.

Although I didn't know it at the time, someone else was also keeping a keen eye on Peggy Fleming: a little twelve-year-old girl named Dorothy Hamill, who went on to Olympic fame of her own eight years later.

When I first saw Dorothy Hamill skate, in the 1976 Winter Olympics in Innsbruck, Austria, she seemed like a completely different kind of figure skater from Peggy Fleming. She appeared a little shorter, a little rounder, and not quite as elegant and exquisite. But the more I watched her, the more I noticed what amazing gifts of her own she had brought to the competition. Dorothy Hamill had great power. Dorothy Hamill had great speed. Dorothy Hamill could jump and leap and twirl and spin like nobody else out there. And Dorothy Hamill had unparalleled charm! She was dynamic, magnetic, thrilling, and loveable—a skater, who could—and did—light up the Innsbruck arena like an Austrian sunrise! Oh, and she also won the gold medal.

Why am I getting into this? Because, here we have two different people, with two very different styles, with two very different strengths, who both managed to achieve the same goal: they won the gold!

This also could be you.

You see, you don't have to possess the same skills or attributes as someone else in order to accomplish the same degree of success. All you have to do is to adapt your own God-given strengths to the task at hand and give it your best. You will be amazed at what you can achieve.

HEEDING THE CALL

Saul of Tarsus hated Christians. His greatest passion was to seek them out, arrest them, drag them back to Jerusalem, and imprison them. Then, with any luck, the proper authorities would execute them. Saul's zeal knew no bounds, and Christians far and wide feared him.

But God had other plans for Saul of Tarsus.

One day, when Saul was traveling to Damascus to seek out more Christians to destroy, he was blinded by a flash of light. "He fell to the ground and heard a voice say to him, 'Saul, Saul, why do you persecute me?' 'Who are you, Lord?' Saul asked. 'I am Jesus, whom you are persecuting,' he replied. 'Now get up and go into the city, and you will be told what you must do'" (Acts 9:4-6).

Those for whom this story is familiar know that Saul went on to become the apostle Paul—often considered the greatest and most influential apostle of them all. His body of work in the New Testament includes the books of Romans, 1 and 2 Corinthians, Galatians, Ephesians, Philippians, Colossians, 1 and

2 Thessalonians, 1 and 2 Timothy, Titus, Philemon, and also, very probably, Hebrews—all this from a man who once would have happily slaughtered all the Christians he could find. How did this happen?

There's an interesting clue in Acts 26, where Paul recalls the story of his conversion while on trial before King Agrippa. He says, "About noon, King Agrippa, as I was on the road, I saw a light from heaven, brighter than the sun, blazing around me and my companions. We all fell to the ground, and I heard a voice saying to me in Aramaic, 'Saul, Saul, why do you persecute me? It is hard for you to kick against the goads'" (Acts 26:13-14).

Here, Jesus is referring to a common method for steering a team of oxen that are pulling a cart. The driver would use a "goad," a long, limber, wooden rod with a sharp tip, to keep the oxen on the path and away from danger. As the oxen were prodded along, they would sometimes protest by kicking back at the goads with their hind legs. Apparently, this is what Saul had been doing to Jesus' attempts to direct him.

What this suggests is that the discomfort we feel in life may be God's way of prodding us toward the path He wants us on—toward the path He created for us to follow. That's why we may not feel "comfortable" with our careers. That's why we may feel rebellious and unsettled: We're being urged to make a course correction. But instead of responding to God, we stubbornly kick back at the goads—which gets us nowhere.

HARNESSED FOR GREATNESS

What is often missed in the story of Saul of Tarsus strikes at the very heart of finding our true, divine, avenue of service. It is important for us to understand that God did not call Saul in order to change his basic character. He called Saul to "harness" him. This angry young man went from being "Saul, Raging Bull of Tarsus" to "Paul, Raging Bull for the Lord." God simply adapted Saul's present strength—the strength he already had—so that Paul could use it for God's glory. He does this with all of us.

Often, I hear people bemoaning their own short-comings and calling these "failings." But they're not. We're not called by God to be changed into something we never were; we're called by God so that He can harness the strengths He has already given us and use them for His glory. There is an old saying: *If you were a bad cook before you became a Christian, you're probably still a bad cook.* It's true. As hard as it may be to believe, we don't need to focus on what we do not have. We need to focus on what we have. That's where our strength is. We already have everything we need to do great things. All we need to do is let God harness us.

ADAPTING YOUR STRENGTH

You may be thinking, "Well, yes, but I'm not young and agile like Peggy Fleming or Dorothy Hamill, and I'm not strong like Saul of Tarsus. In fact, I am getting up in years and I don't know if I have anything left to 'harness.'"

It's easy to feel this way.

But the fact is, God tells us, "Go in the strength you *have*," not "Go in the strength you *used to* have." In other words, God can use us at any stage of our lives, if we are willing.

If we are willing.

Corrie ten Boom shares a wonderful story in her book *Tramp for the Lord* about a time when she visited Lithuania, which at the time was still part of the Soviet Union. There she met with an elderly man and woman, a Christian couple, who lived in a tiny one-room upstairs apartment, in relative isolation from the Communist world below. The woman's body had been ravaged by multiple sclerosis, and she was twisted and bent almost beyond recognition. Most of her muscles had atrophied to the point of uselessness, but she was still able to manage a warm smile for her guests. Next to the old woman's couch was a vintage typewriter. Each day, every day, the woman's husband propped her up on the couch between two pillows, and the woman would slowly, methodically, and painfully type out Christian literature, using just one gnarled finger. Ten Boom writes: "All day and far into the night she would type. She translated Christian books into Russian, Latvian, and the language of her people. Always using just that one finger—peck . . . peck . . . peck—she typed out the pages. Portions of the Bible, the books of Billy Graham, Watchman Nee, and Corrie ten Boom—all came from her typewriter."[4]

Sensing Corrie's anguish and despair as she observed the woman laboring over the typewriter, the
husband soothingly revealed that he believed God
had a purpose in his wife's illness. He said, "Every
other Christian in this city is watched by the secret
police; but she has been sick so long that no one ever
looks in on her."

That is *going in the strength you have.*

STRENGTH "ON THE SIDE"

In the book business, we like to say, "There are no new
ideas, only new treatments"—that is, only new ways of
expressing old ideas.

That's what you are: a new treatment. You have your
own particular insights, your own fascinating angles.
You have your own unique methods and your own
singular strategies. You have your own special ways of
doing things. When you take these strengths into the
world—and use them—great things can happen.

I would like to offer one caution, though: There
will always be some people who do not appreciate, admire, or understand your unique qualities or abilities.
Throughout my career, I have read a lot of criticism
about my children's books: too syrupy, too preachy,
too didactic, too predictable . . . and so forth. This
criticism has always reminded me of what people
used to say about the great comedy team of Laurel
and Hardy: "Nobody liked them but the public."

I think that's hilarious. While the critics have
found many things to wrinkle their noses about in

my books, the public has bought millions of them. It's a lesson worth noting and remembering.

It's also worth noting that I continued to work in corporate America for more than twenty years after I sold my first book. Despite how fabulously wealthy everyone assumes authors are, it turns out that only a small percent can live on their royalties alone. The rest need to supplement their income with a "day job." That was true for me. The good news is that this is where I learned to use my strength "on the side."

As I mentioned earlier, I didn't originally set out to write children's books. I actually intended to write the Great American Novel. To accomplish this, I left my retail job—where my working hours were haphazard and irregular—and found a job where I could work a standard forty-hour workweek. I figured this would allow me to establish a regular and set time each evening to work on my masterpiece. This decision eventually led to my taking a job with the Lockheed Aircraft Corporation in Burbank, California, where I worked in the aforementioned underground bunker for the next three years.

I was hired as a project scheduler. My job was to create "recovery schedules" for the assembly-line managers to follow when they fell behind on installing some segment of the planes they were putting together. I had no experience in any of this—but it didn't matter. I was a fresh pair of arms and legs, and that was good enough, I guess.

When you do work for the government, as Lockheed

does, there tends to be a lot of downtime, a lot of waiting around, a lot of time to kill while contracts are being negotiated and implemented. To fill this void, I started carrying a little notebook in my back pocket and making notes for my novel as new ideas came to me. In other words, I started using my strength "on the side." When people asked me, "P.K., what do you do here?" I answered, "I'm a project scheduler." Then I would quickly add, somewhat confidentially, "But really I'm a writer!" And as strange as it may seem, nobody ever questioned this. Nobody ever said, "Oh yeah? What have you written?" Instead, they would say, "Oh yeah? Would you mind writing my paper?" or "Would you mind writing my speech?" or "Would you mind writing my proposal to the US government?" And so forth. Within a matter of months, I became the unofficial head writer of the manufacturing division—which was ludicrous, because I couldn't write for beans! But it turns out that the whole world steps aside for someone who seems to know what he or she is doing.

Anyway, this set the standard for the rest of my time in corporate America. No matter where I went, or what I was hired to do, I always told people I was a writer, and I always ended up doing the company's writing. I wrote speeches. I wrote articles. I wrote brochures. I wrote advertising and promotional copy. I wrote tech manuals. I wrote scripts. I wrote everything. It was during this time that I truly honed my skills. By using my strength "on the side" for twenty years, I finally was able to move it to the forefront.

This could be true for you, too. You may not be able to find a job that fits your strength. That's okay. Let your strength fit your job. In time, your true calling will emerge. There's no stopping it: *After all, is God not sending you?*

A GOOD ATTITUDE

For the past thirty-five years, I have taught a ten-week class (now an all-day seminar) called Writing Picture Books for Children. I structured my teaching around the acronym ASPIRE, which stands for Attitude, Skill, Presentation, Information, Reach, and Energy. *Attitude* refers to how highly or lowly you think of yourself. *Skill* refers to how well you have developed your craft. *Presentation* refers to the appearance, content, and accuracy of your manuscript, cover letter, and other written materials. *Information* covers the basics of a publishing contract, including advances, royalties, subsidiary rights, copyright, and so forth. *Reach* refers to giving your book greater exposure— greater *reach* into the marketplace—by using various forms of personal marketing, such as newspaper press releases, bookstore book signings, and local TV appearances. Finally, *Energy* refers to not giving up just because you're tired. Of the above six elements, I consider a good *attitude* to be 90 percent of a writer's success. I like to say that a bad writer with a good attitude will always be more successful than a good writer with a bad attitude. In other words, what you think about yourself—what you think about your strengths—is crucial. More often than not, people are far more critical of themselves than anyone else is. That's why it's important to remember that God does not make mistakes. He created us and He is very pleased with His creation. To the best of our ability, we need to see ourselves through God's eyes. He loves us so much that He died for us—for each of us, *personally*. (That should put a bounce in your step and a smile on your face.) We need to overcome, even fight against, the negative feelings about ourselves, which are not from God. They are from the other guy, the one who relishes our misery and our failure. We cannot let his negativity take us captive. Everything he whispers in our ears is a lie from the pit of hell. Let's deny him the pleasure and send him packing!

Keeping a positive attitude about ourselves is extremely helpful in anything we want to accomplish.

Five Tips to Grow By

I would like to offer five tips that I have found useful for anyone who desires and seeks to *go in the strength they have*. They are:

1. Declare yourself.

Whether you're a writer, a dancer, a bookkeeper, or a circus clown, it helps to declare yourself to others. Whenever I teach would-be writers, I always encourage them to have business cards and stationery made up with their name on it, followed by their title—Writer—whether or not they've attempted to write professionaly yet. I also encourage them to set up an office, or a work area, as soon as they can and to begin keeping track of their expenses, just like other writers do. In other words, I encourage them to act as if it were already so—as if they are already the real deal, the genuine article, that they are seeking to be. Finally, I encourage them to tell their family and friends—and total strangers—that they are writers. This helps them to accept in their own hearts that it's true. The more we speak about, and do about, a life goal, the more that goal becomes a reality.

2. Focus.

It is often the case that a person has several strengths. I have named this the "Mason Williams Syndrome." Back in the late 1960s, there was a television show called *The Smothers Brothers Comedy Hour.* One of the Smothers Brothers' regular guests was Mason Williams, an entertainer who played classical guitar, twelve-string guitar, and banjo. His most famous work is a delightful instrumental called "Classical Gas." Mason Williams is good at almost everything he does. He performs classical music, bluegrass music, folk music, and easy-listening music. He is a lyricist, a poet, and an accomplished comedy writer, and he has published several books. But what I remember most about Mason Williams is that I could not figure what he was. I didn't know where to put him. I didn't know how to cheer for him. I always thought that if he had chosen just one of his strengths to focus on, he might have been considerably more . . . well, famous.

This is true for many people.

Artists in particular have this problem. Virtually every artist I know is multitalented. If they can write, they can sing. If they can sculpt, they can dance. If they can paint, they can play the guitar . . . and so forth. This can be a personal blessing, but a career curse. The principle at work here is akin to the old expression, "A jack of all trades, but master of none"; that is, the more we spread our strength around, the more we diffuse it.

Returning to my writing students for a moment, I always ask them to focus on only one genre of literature in their writing. Though they usually take my class to learn how to write children's books—because it looks like so much fun—it turns out that most of them are, frankly, better suited to other forms of writing. There are two general rules for writers: write what you like to read, and write what you know about. The first rule is easy: If you like to read romance novels, you should probably write romance novels. The second rule is easy, too: Don't write detective novels set in Paris if you have no clue how detectives work and you've never been to France.

My advice is this: if you are multi-gifted and good at doing a whole lot of things, simply move toward the one area you enjoy the most. This is where your real strength lies and this is where you will find your greatest reward.

3. Imagine yourself successful.

Although "success" can mean different things to different people, I would like to use it here simply to mean the evidence that a goal has been achieved. When I first started writing children's books full-time, back in 1988, I was living in San Diego. In daydreaming about the impact I would someday make on the children's book world, I envisioned people in New York City standing on a sidewalk outside a bookstore, staring through its plate glass window at one of my books. Within only a couple of years, I started getting fan mail from New York City. What I learned from this experience was that all accomplishments begin with a picture that forms in our minds. For example, if we are planning to go to Hawaii, we first envision ourselves on the beach at Waikiki, having a wonderful day in the surf and sand. Then we envision purchasing the airline ticket, getting on the plane, and stepping out of the plane into the warm, balmy air of Oahu. Often, by the time we set foot on the tarmac, we sense an eerie déjà vu—as if we've done this before. This same sensation occurs when we daydream—or pray about—where we want our lives to take us. We suddenly see people staring through plate glass windows at our creation—and it seems eerily familiar.

4. Invite feedback.

It never hurts to seek the opinion of others about the work we are doing. In fact, the Bible says, "Plans fail for lack of counsel, but with many advisers they succeed" (Proverbs 15:22).

Returning for a moment to my friend Spencer Johnson, I remember when he finished his first draft of *The One-Minute Manager*. Before he went any further with it, he sent copies of the manuscript to fifty people—the people whose opinions he respected the most—and asked them to mark up any changes they would like to see and return the manuscripts to him. Spencer then gathered the returned, marked-up copies and implemented as many of the suggested changes as he could. His theory was that, in doing this one simple thing, he would have at least fifty people who liked his book when it finally came out on the market. It was a great plan. Of all the people I have known in my forty-plus years of writing, Spencer has probably the greatest flair for marketing both himself and his work. I believe he is a true genius (and one who works hard).

Sometimes, critical feedback is difficult to receive. This is where personal humility can be vitally important. Humility, often defined as "strength under control," is all-powerful because it cannot be toppled. It's like shadowboxing. You can swing all you want, but you can't knock down a truly humble person. You're just flailing the air.

Though I appreciate feedback, I will confess to not wanting it during my creative process. I've found that negative comments, right or wrong, seem to take root, while positive comments quickly evaporate and drift away. Negative comments can handcuff me to a degree, because I tend to focus too much on the criticism and not enough on the body of work before me. Frankly, even some positive comments can throw me off my game, because they also demand too much attention. However, when I'm finished, it's a different story. Although receptiveness to feedback took a long time to develop in my character, I now will listen very carefully to what people feel motivated to tell me about my work—whether it is about writing and illustrating children's books, preaching a sermon, or running a small church. I've learned to listen with my heart and not my head. I choose to believe that people generally have my best interests in mind, so I do what I can to receive their comments—no matter how wigged out they may seem at first. In this way, I have forced myself to remain teachable, and this has paid wonderful dividends.

5. Hang around with others who share your interests.

A few years back, at a church I was visiting, I asked a young Christian man what he wanted to do with his life. Much to my delight, he told me he wanted to direct motion pictures. I say "much to my delight" because, frankly, I've grown weary of Christians who believe the only right answer to this question is: "I'm thinking of going into full-time ministry." To amplify this, let me quickly say that I will never forget what a friend of mine—a woman who worked at a local Christian bookstore—told me when I shared with her that I deeply regretted having stepped down as pastor of my first church. When I told her I felt as if I had let God down, she looked up at me, smiled warmly, and said, "You know, P.K., we Christians need a few heroes we can look up to." This hit me hard. What she was saying was: "We Christians need a few role models other than pastors." I completely agree. I think of football great Kurt Warner and how much I enjoyed watching his success over the years. I think of Charles Schulz, who made certain that the finished version of *A Charlie Brown Christmas* contained Linus's recitation of Luke 2:8-14, which begins: "And there were in the same country shepherds abiding in the field, keeping watch over their flock by night" (KJV). I think of Tim Tebow, George Foreman, Pat Boone, Randy Travis, George Bush, and all the other high-profile Christians who have not been afraid to publicly name Jesus Christ as their Lord and Savior. My bookstore friend was right: We Christians do need a few heroes we can look up to.

Anyway, I told this young Christian man who wanted to be a director that I thought he should move to Hollywood, because that's where he would find the most people who could help him along his career path. In one form or another, I tell everyone to get close to others who are already doing the type of work they want to do. It's my "Greenwich Village" approach to success, where gifted people hang out together, encouraging one another, and sometimes even pulling each other along as they step up into success.

When I lived in San Diego, particularly during the mid-1980s, I often attended gatherings with other children's authors. These get-togethers included school visits, book signings, author teas, regional and national booksellers' conventions, and anything else people could come up with. The event I remember best was a weeklong "reading festival" in Bakersfield, which consisted of five full days of frantic and endless school visits. Each morning, we were picked up at our hotel and driven to local elementary schools, where we gave a one-hour presentation about four times. This was exhausting, to say the least. It was so bad, in fact, that one evening, sitting around a dinner table with my fellow authors, we coined the phrase "author abuse," which said it all. The event ran us ragged, but the camaraderie was worth every second.

Joining me at these events were people who went on to do some truly great things in the children's book industry: Laura Numeroff, who wrote *If You Give a Mouse a Cookie*; Barney Saltzberg, author of *Beautiful Oops!*; John Archambault, who coauthored *Chicka Chicka Boom Boom*; Pam Munoz Ryan, author of *When Marian Sang*; and April Halprin Wayland, who wrote *Girl Coming in for a Landing*. And this is just the short list of titles for these talented authors. Whether we inspired one another is anyone's guess, but I think it's noteworthy that we've all done well in our children's book careers. My advice? Get as close as you can to other people who share your interests. It's amazing how high-octane enthusiasm rubs off.

The young would-be movie director never did go to Hollywood. He decided to stay closer to home and be "more realistic" about his future. Too bad. But that's how it goes. Wishing is always easier than doing.

Finally, one other observation about my five tips: When I declared myself ("I am a children's writer"), focused my God-given strength on that one task, imagined myself successful, invited feedback, and hung around with others who shared my interests, suddenly it was as if the entire universe rallied to support me. Opportunities came out of nowhere. Doors opened that had always been closed. My life changed so quickly I could hardly keep up with it. Before I even realized it, I was immersed in the world of children's authors and illustrators. It had all started with a thought, a daydream; but suddenly I was in the thick of it—and it seemed eerily familiar.

GLEANING FROM OTHERS

Just because you are setting out to accomplish something "original" does not mean we cannot glean from others who have gone before us. In the ministry, we call this attitude "standing on the shoulders of the saints." Although many modern-day Americans like to believe that we human beings finally have arrived at a period of enlightenment, I am convinced this is just egotistical nonsense. There have been many brilliant minds over the centuries, whose profound insights, writings, and opinions are invaluable. We need to pay attention to these people; no one has a lock on clear thinking.

In any career—not just in the ministry—there are people who can offer us invaluable insights and standards. It pays to study these role models.

I have never made it a secret that the people who influenced me the most in my children's book career were Dr. Seuss, Norman Rockwell, and Charles Schulz.

Dr. Seuss influenced me, not only because of his amazing and charming ability to rhyme but also because of the types of topics he occasionally chose to tackle. I specifically was moved by *The Grinch Who Stole Christmas* and *The Lorax*. Both books focused on important social issues, which motivated me, over time, to latch onto my "find a hole and fill it" motif for my children's books.

I admire Norman Rockwell because of how he created so much *movement* and *interaction* in his art. In a Norman Rockwell painting, someone is always peeking at someone; or something is about to happen; or something just *did* happen; or there is an imminent collision of some kind. I love it. When I create my art, I try to pour in the same kinds of living interactions as Rockwell did. This is why the first thing I draw for any new children's book page is my main character's face. If his expression captures the mood I'm trying to convey, if his eyes lead the viewer to the "imminent collision" or "secret collusion" between characters, then the rest of the drawing, no matter how many other characters are in it, is a piece of cake. In any case, I believe Norman Rockwell was a genius—oddly underappreciated in his time—and I continue to admire his unique ability to capture the essence of people and life. In fact, only about a foot away from me on my desk as I write this book is a little pewter paperweight of Norman Rockwell's famous painting of himself painting himself as a self-portrait. It is hilarious, and I smile every time I look at it.

Then there is Charles Schulz—"Sparky" to his friends—who probably has influenced me most of all. I was a very poor reader as a child, mildly dyslexic, and I chose to read Peanuts books instead of longer, more difficult works, like, say, *War and Peace*. As a result, when I started illustrating my books, the characters I drew looked vaguely like Charlie Brown and Company. Frankly, I never noticed this until I began visiting elementary schools, and the kids started screaming, "Charlie Brown! Charlie Brown!" whenever I drew my own character—Little P.K.—on an art tablet, right before their eyes. After a while, whenever someone told me—cheerfully—that my characters reminded them of Peanuts, my heart sank. So one day, I sent Charles Schulz one of my children's books with an accompanying letter explaining the unintended similarity of my art to his—and how sorry I was. A few weeks later, I received a letter back from him. It was one of the most gracious letters I have ever read. In essence, he said he felt I had my own "unique style" and I should be very proud of the work I was doing. I was touched. In a sense, though, his observation was not only gracious, it was correct. Here's what I mean: I had sent him a copy of my book *Today Is Halloween*, which contains some of the best artwork I have ever done. Since the whole book takes place at night, all the illustrations were painted originally in "daylight" colors and then slowly darkened to achieve the effect of evening. The result is a celebration of light and shadow that took me forever to create and truly captures the tone and feel of All Hallows Eve. This is where Peanuts and I part company: in the use and application of color. I like to tell elementary school kids that I'm not a good "draw-er" but that I am a very good "color-er-er-er-er." I say it just like this, too—with four extra "ers"—and the kids always squeal with delight. But this is true. Coloring is one of my God-given strengths, so I have taken it into battle with me.

THE OPERATIVE WORD

Though I have focused primarily on our natural and unique gifts in this section of the book, there is one other aspect of the Lord's instruction to Gideon that I briefly want to discuss. You'll recall that the Angel of the Lord says to Gideon, "Go in the strength you have." The operative word here is *go*.

It didn't matter that Gideon already possessed all the strength God was looking for. It was imperative that Gideon *use* it. Yes, he hemmed and hawed and sputtered and stalled, but eventually he took his strength into battle for the Lord. We all need to do this. We may be the world's greatest cook, but if we never open the kitchen door and bring out the tray, we are depriving the rest of the world of the blessing of our gift. And that's the primary reason God gave us our gifts: to be a blessing to others and, thereby, to glorify Him.

On the west shore of the Sea of Galilee, probably in Capernaum, Jesus healed a woman who had been hemorrhaging for twelve long, painful, years. Immediately following this healing, Jesus continued walking with a local synagogue ruler, a man named Jairus, who earlier had pleaded with Him to come to his home to heal his dying twelve-year-old daughter. At this point, some men from Jairus's home approach and say to the synagogue ruler, "Your daughter is dead . . . Why bother the teacher anymore?" But Jesus ignores these words and says to Jairus, "Don't be afraid; just believe" (see Mark 5:21–36).

Words to live by. Jesus says these same words of encouragement to us whenever the doomsayers approach and try to steal our hope. There are always plenty of people who will tell us that something can't be done—that we're too old, that the opportunity is past, that we're wasting our time, and so forth. They say, "Why bother anymore?" But Jesus says, "Don't be afraid; just believe."

And, He adds: *After all, am I not sending you?*

By the way, Jesus healed Jairus's daughter.

STEP ONE:
WORK HARD

STEP TWO:
GO IN THE STRENGTH
YOU HAVE

FINISH WHAT YOU START

There are many beginnings, but few endings.
CHINESE PROVERB

*They went to a place called Gethsemane, and Jesus
said to his disciples, "Sit here while I pray." He took
Peter, James and John along with him, and he began to
be deeply distressed and troubled. "My soul is overwhelmed with sorrow to the point of death," he said
to them. "Stay here and keep watch." Going a little
farther, he fell to the ground and prayed that if possible
the hour might pass from him. "Abba, Father," he said,
"everything is possible for you. Take this cup from me."*
MARK 14:32–36

QUITTING TOO SOON

Several years ago, a nationally syndicated magazine
asked one hundred of the most successful people in
America why so many others failed at their chosen endeavors. The answer was unanimous: "They quit too
soon."

When I do a book signing at a mall, or at some
other highly populated venue, often a long line of
people will form to wait for my autograph and my

personal inscription to them or to their children. As they wait, they are usually lined up alongside a narrow display table loaded with my various titles. Even though they have already chosen the book, or books, they want to purchase, they normally will browse the other books as they slowly move past them. Invariably, at some point, I will scan down the line and see one person who is flipping through my books—trying to appear curious about them—but with no real interest at all. And my heart sinks, because I always know what this person wants.

When this person gets to the head of the line, he or she will always ask me the same question. Always. It may come in several variations, but the gist of the question is this: "Can you tell me how to get a book published?" Now, as I mentioned earlier, I used to teach a ten-week class at the University of California in San Diego on this very subject. Ten weeks. Ten *long* weeks. So trying to answer this question in the time available during a crowded book signing—which is about one minute per person—is not only difficult, it is impossible. For years, however, I tried to answer it anyway—because I like to be a good guy—and I would rattle off as much information as I could while I signed the book, a book this person did not really want to buy in the first place.

One day, I got smart.

The next time it happened, I politely asked, "Have you finished a manuscript yet?" Guess what the answer was? Guess what the answer *always* is. You're right. The answer was *no*. It's always no. So I said, "Here's what I will do: I'm in the phone book. When you finish your manuscript, call me, and I will tell you everything I know about getting your book published." Guess how many phone calls I have received over the past twenty-five years, from the hundreds of people who have asked me this question. Right again. None. Not any. Never. Nil. To my knowledge, no one who has ever asked me how to get a book published has finished a manuscript.

This has been equally true of the many students I have taught over the years in my class, Writing Picture Books for Children. I estimate I have coached about four thousand men and women on every aspect I know about creating, writing, illustrating, publishing, and marketing a children's book. But to my knowledge, only one—*one!*—ever actually finished a manuscript and went on to get it published. I was discouraged by this until I realized that my job was not to help my students get published. My job was to feed their dreams. That was the true reason most of them were taking my class. They just loved the whole fantasy of writing children's books and becoming famous. They didn't care as much for the reality. This was when I first discovered the concept of Wishers and Doers that I described in Step One.

I have an older brother named Tim, who has written and published about fourteen detective novels. He and I agree that more people would be published if they would just finish their manuscripts. Besides the obvious problem that no one can get a book published without a finished manuscript, accomplishing this task alone puts a person in the ninety-ninth percentile of all writers currently living in America.

People just don't finish things.

MOVE IN TO STAY

In his book about Mother Teresa, *Something Beautiful for God*, author Malcolm Muggeridge puts the phenomenon of quitting too soon a little differently. He was staying in Calcutta in order to interview Mother Teresa for the book he wanted to write. One evening, when he was being driven through the overcrowded streets of the city, his driver accidently hit a pedestrian. Keenly aware of how dangerous the situation could become, the driver quickly picked up the injured person and drove him at top speed to the nearest hospital. Muggeridge describes the hospital waiting room as a place of unimaginable horror, with injured bodies scattered all around the floor, and one man staggering in whose throat just had been cut from ear to ear. At this point, Muggeridge raced back to his hotel room for a stiff whiskey and soda, and soon left Calcutta, vowing to make certain that the proper authorities did something about the city's wretched social conditions—someday. He writes, "I ran away and stayed away. Mother Teresa moved in and stayed. That was the difference."[5]

I appreciate Muggeridge's honesty. One of the most important keys to success in anything is to *move in to stay.* Whatever we are striving for, whatever we are working toward, whatever we are trying to accomplish—at some point—we must move in to stay. We must close the back door. We must remove the escape route. We must dismiss the other options. As a businessperson, as a teacher, as a parent, as a spouse . . . whatever; if we want to see fruit from our labors, sooner or later we must stop dabbling and make firm commitments to the tasks directly in front of us. This makes all the difference.

HONOR YOUR WORD

I feel called to add that "finishing what we start" includes keeping our word. I am constantly amazed at how lightly people take the act of promising to do something. "I will be there." "I am coming." "You can count on me." None of these apparently means anything to a whole slew of otherwise good and godly folks. At least when someone tells me, "I will try to be there," I know what they mean. They mean they are not coming. One of my favorite examples of doing what you say you will do comes from the story of the Prodigal Son (see Luke 15:11-32). Here we have a young man who has demanded his inheritance from his father—while his father is still alive, no less—and then goes out and squanders it all on worldly pleasures. Sounds like a lot of people I know. But here's the deal: He eventually finds himself standing in pig slop—regretting his terrible choices—and decides to go back home to his father and say, "Father, I have sinned against heaven and against you. I am no longer worthy to be called your son." And guess what? That's exactly what he does. He goes back to the family home, where, much to his surprise, his father runs to greet him and gives him a great big bear hug. The son then takes two steps backward and says to his father, "Father, I have sinned against heaven and against you. I am no longer worthy to be called your son." Good for him. I really like this. He actually did what he said he would do. It's fortunate he hadn't said that he would *try* to tell his father these things, or it wouldn't have happened.

Honoring our word is not only basic to business, it is basic to life. Doing what we say we are going to do, keeping our promises, meeting our deadlines . . . all these help others to believe in us. Woody Allen has been quoted as saying, "Ninety percent of life is just showing up." I would like to amend this to say, "Ninety percent of life is just showing up—if you have said you will show up." My version is not as catchy, but it makes my point.

Suppose, for example, that God decided not to honor *His* Word. The Bible tells us, "All of God's promises have been fulfilled in Christ with a resounding 'Yes!'" (2 Corinthians 1:20 NLT). But what if this Scripture read, "*Most of* God's promises have been fulfilled in Christ . . . maybe"? What if Jesus had said, "Lo, I will *try* to be with you always, even to the end of the age"? Or what if He had told His disciples, "I will *try* never to leave you or forsake you"? You see what happens? That little bit of hedging undoes the whole value and reliability of the promises. Which leaves us where? It leaves us nowhere. It leaves us right back where we were before we ever heard of, or believed in, the Word of God. It leaves us lost in the darkness once more.

We must honor our word. It's a shame we even need to remind ourselves of this. There was a time when a person's word was all that was needed to bind a legal contract. People gave their word, shook hands, and that was the end of it. And so it should be.

WHY PEOPLE QUIT

There are endless reasons why people give up on a dream. I don't pretend to know all of them—or even most of them—but I have seen, and even experienced, several of them. The following, then, is only a partial list of the reasons that people throw in the towel instead of finishing what they have started.

1. Fantasy vs. Reality

My wife, Jeanne, quickly dismisses many of life's disappointments by simply saying, "Fantasy, reality." She says it just like that—without a verb—and I know what she means. She means that the reality of a person's dream has not lived up to, or even approximated, the fantasy that person had in mind. This is a very common problem.

Consider a pretty young girl who dreams of being a movie star. It seems like such an exciting and wonderful life, with people fussing over you everywhere you go and fans cheering wildly from the sidewalks as you drive by in your limousine. There are the television interviews. There are the red carpet receptions. There are opening nights. There are even the Academy Awards, where you get to thank everyone— from your agent, to your director, to your producer— without whose help you would not be standing in front of the cameras receiving this award. Finally, there are the tears of joy as you are led away backstage by another beautiful young woman whose dream *did not* come true.

And then there is the reality.

I think of Marilyn Monroe, dead at thirty-six. I think of Judy Garland, married five times and dead at forty-seven. I think of Margaux Hemingway, dead at forty-two. I even think of Elizabeth Taylor, who lived to be seventy-nine but was married eight times. I think of all the actresses who have been miserably unhappy in their careers. There are the years of waiting tables just to survive. There are the endless auditions with the endless rejections. There are the constant come-ons from Hollywood bigwigs. There are bit parts, throwaway parts, and parts on the cutting room floor. And there are the ever-available solicitations from seedy characters who would like you to star in "adult" films.

But maybe, just maybe, there is also the big break. This often leads to a whole new set of problems. There may be hours, even days, of boredom and inactivity spent in a trailer, or on the set, between takes. There may be an army of powerful—and lecherous—producers, directors, and established male movie stars to ward off—or worse yet, to accede to. There may be a lousy script. The movie might be a bomb. The reviewers might be scathing and merciless. Often, when an actress is too pretty, she is haughtily dismissed by the press as dumb and talentless. If this happens, she may become the scapegoat for the lousy film, making new roles very difficult to find.

Or—the movie just might be a hit, and she might become a "star."

This, of course, can create yet another painful set of realities. Suddenly, the paparazzi are everywhere! Suddenly, every step she takes is being photographed, scrutinized, sensationalized, lied about, and trashed. Suddenly, she cannot just stop for a cup of coffee at Starbucks. She cannot just enjoy a nice lunch with a friend at Applebee's. She cannot even pick up her prescription at the Wal-Mart pharmacy. Her privacy is ripped away from her by complete strangers, forcing her to live in hiding, like a vampire, away from the windows, away from the backyard, and away from the light.

What began as a beautiful dream has been twisted into a garish nightmare.

Although this scenario may be a bit over the top, it points out how different a fantasy can be from the ensuing reality. Perhaps this was true of former president George W. Bush. Although it is fashionable among some in this country to treat George Bush with haughty contempt and ridicule, I happen to like him very much. In fact, I grieve at the way he has been routinely butchered and skewered by Hollywood and the media. They treat him like a piñata at a child's birthday party. Anyway, though I don't remember the date or the occasion, I will always remember something he said one afternoon when he was speaking in front of an assemblage of news reporters on the White House lawn. In response to a critical remark, President Bush smiled, shook his head, and said, "Being president of the United States is hard. It's a hard job." As much as I like George Bush, I had to laugh. First, it was the way he said hard. It was more Texas-like, as in "haurred." But it was also just the obviousness of the statement. Of course being president of the United States is a hard job! It is the most powerful and important job in the world! And it flashed across my mind as I was listening to him: Didn't you know this about the office before you ran? I'm sure he had a good idea of what he was getting into, but it's easy to underestimate the difficulties of realizing any given fantasy. I still like him anyway.

I can easily give you other examples of this kind of mismatch. Some people dream of opening a bed-and-breakfast, but after they do, they hate it. They quickly find out that there are a lot of people who are rude—and just as many who are slobs. So they go back to working for Sears. There are people who open a store, only to find out that they don't like working with the public. My late father-in-law is a prime example of this. He opened a little downtown restaurant, a coffee shop actually, in a New Jersey town and quickly learned that he hated all the policemen and firemen who expected to get free coffee and donuts every day. There was also a drunk who staggered into his restaurant one morning and fell down the basement steps, nearly killing himself. It was a good thing this happened before people started suing everybody else for their own mistakes. My wife and her brothers always refer to their father's coffee shop as "Smungy's." This was not the real name, but nobody can remember what the real name was.

The wisest advice I can offer here is to be practical about your fantasies, so that when reality finally rears its ugly head, you are at least somewhat prepared for the shock and can respond with fierce determination—and keep going.

2. Feelings of Inadequacy

Another reason that people abandon their dreams is because they feel inadequate—or ill-prepared—for the task they've chosen. Well, here's the good news: We all feel this way. At the beginning of a career, everyone feels like a fake. This was true of me as a children's author and again as a pastor. There's a good reason for this. When we first begin something, we *are* fakes; it's the only way we can possibly approach any new endeavor. We pretend to be the thing that we are, hoping to convince others that we are what we say we are. In time, however, the pretense becomes more of a reality, and the feelings of phoniness slowly subside. Now that I have written and illustrated more than ninety children's books, I feel like a real children's author. But it did not start out this way. I probably spent ten years hoping that nobody would come along and expose me for the fraud I really was.

I suspect these feelings are equally true in every occupation.

Doctors spend eight years in medical school, studying night and day, losing hours of sleep, struggling to learn the complexities of their craft. But I have no doubts that when their first patient walks into the examination room, the doctor is a nervous wreck. If the doctor is male, I imagine he lowers his voice a little to seem more seasoned and professional. If the doctor is female, I would guess she adjusts her posture a bit to seem more confident and in charge. In other words, they are both acting. They are putting on a show so that they will appear like their preconceived images of what doctors are supposed to appear like. And God bless them for it. They fooled me.

What I am laboring over is this: The moment we choose a career for ourselves, for all practical purposes we become the real thing—whether or not we *feel* like it. I have been a pastor for more than fifteen years now, and I still don't feel like a real pastor. This may have to do with my success in the kiddy book business or my lifelong battles with grandiosity, but that's really not the point. The point is I don't have to BE the real thing to DO the real thing. It's that simple.

It is also helpful to consider the legend of the young Greek soldier in combat who broke his sword and fled the battlefield. Soon, another young soldier came along, picked up the broken sword, and with that sword turned the tide of the battle. In other words, it's not what you have in your hand that matters, it's how you *use* what you have in your hand.

More words to live by: "But as for you, be strong and do not give up, for your work will be rewarded" (2 Chronicles 15:7). This is a promise from God. And God keeps His Word.

3. Little or No Fruit

One of the more discouraging problems we can have in our chosen endeavors is a lack of "fruit"—evidence that we're accomplishing anything. This is very common. Whatever we do, we naturally want to see results. If I'm a car salesman, I want to see a lot of cars sold. If I'm a waiter, I want to see nice tips for my troubles. If I own a bed-and-breakfast, I want to see all the rooms full. If I'm a farmer, I want to see a good harvest. And so forth. More often than not, people measure their worth, or their skill, by the response they get from others. Often, when there is little or no response to what we do, a sense of pointlessness and failure can set in. If this continues for too long, thoughts of surrendering, of throwing in the towel, of walking away, of just plain quitting are all too real.

But this may be the wrong thing to do.

Although, relatively speaking, I have been quite successful in my children's book career—and have received more than my share of positive strokes—this has not been true in my life as a pastor. In fact, my life as a pastor has born little visible fruit. And it has taken me years to find out why.

I became the pastor of my first church when the pastor I was assisting was given a larger church in the northern part of our state. As strange as it may seem, I was offered the position of pastor even though I had been a Christian for only eighteen months. Practically, and biblically, this was a bad idea. Everyone just assumed—because of my ability to stand in and preach for the real pastor—that I could move into the role rather seamlessly. My own pastor later told me that he knew it would be difficult for me, but he had encouraged me to do it anyway because he wanted it to serve as a form of "Bible college" for me. In any case, the whole enterprise was only one step short of disaster. The strife, the turmoil, the infighting, the criticism . . . all of it just about killed me. And after four years, I'd had enough. When I stepped down, I felt like an abject failure.

My second attempt at pastoring a church came two years later, when again I was asked to take over for a pastor who had moved on. This church, which was located about 250 miles north of my home, was in complete disarray, both structurally and financially, and had an odd array of parishioners.

Although these things were challenging, to say the least, they were not the reason I stepped down a few months later. There is an old admonition among pastors that goes: "Don't try to export a ministry that's not working at home." The real problem for me was that my wife didn't want to move away from Ashland. At first I thought she would be okay with it, but after looking at about 117 homes for sale—none of which met with Jeanne's approval—I realized she was never going to find a home she liked because she didn't *want* to find a home she liked. So I buttoned things up and left this church, too.

My third church is the church I now pastor. It is called Joy Chapel Christian Fellowship and is located in downtown Ashland, across the street from beautiful Lithia Park, in an old gray-and-white building known as the Community Center. I have been there now for four years and I am happy to say that this is where I finally found out what it means to be a pastor.

The congregation has grown little, if at all, since I founded this small church. No matter what we do, we have about two dozen people. If two new members come in, two older members go out. For the first three years, this really bothered me.

People who are not in the ministry are quick to say, "Everyone is in your church whom God wants there." And pastors of megachurches like to say, "Don't focus on the empty seats; focus on the full ones." And I get it. But these platitudes do little to help a pastor whose church refuses to grow—year after year—even up to the dismal national average of forty-five members. We all want evidence that we are doing a good job. In the ministry, *people* are the evidence. Here is how bad it can get: A pastor-friend told me about a dream he had where he was preaching from the pulpit, and every time he looked up from his notes, fewer people were sitting in the pews. This kept happening until, when he looked up for about the fifth time, only his wife was left sitting in the church. And the next time he looked up, even she was gone.

I know exactly how he feels.

But to paraphrase George W. Bush, "Being a pastor is *haurred* work!"

Most people have no idea how difficult it is to write a sermon. Usually, I spend all week long thinking about it, making notes about it, and then writing it. When I step up brightly to the pulpit each Sunday and see the same two dozen faces looking at me—along with the thirty empty chairs that we always optimistically put out just in case—my confidence droops. I liken this to preparing a huge feast each week, setting and decorating a magnificent and elegant table, and then having about three people straggle in to eat. This can be discouraging, to say the least.

Until you find out why.

You see, I always assumed that God called me into the ministry because I'm such a great speaker. Public speaking is the easiest thing in the world for me, and it always has been. I remember as far back as second grade entertaining the other kids with my stand-up comedy. "When I was born, I was such an ugly baby that the doctor slapped my mother." (Thank you, Rodney Dangerfield.) As a children's author, I have spoken all over America—and generally I am a real crowd-pleaser. In fact, I'm a real crowd-pleaser as a preacher, too. But here's the problem: that's not why the Lord called me into the ministry. Believe it or not, He called me to take care of His people—not to entertain them.

He has kept my church small for two reasons: He knew if He grew my church, I would take all the credit (I would have assumed that my irrepressible charm had done it all), and only in a small church can you truly find out how much God's people are hurting. I like to say that if *my* church is any indication of other congregations, then every person, in every congregation in the world, is suffering. This is why they need Jesus. This is why they need a pastor. This is why they need me. And this is why we need each other. Life hurts.

Why am I telling you all this? Because you, like me, might be bearing fruit and not even know it. You might be so focused on what you think God *should* be doing with your life that you're missing what He *is* doing with your life. It happens all the time.

In the mid-1800s, Robert Moffat, a former missionary to South Africa, visited Scotland in order to find some new recruits to help him with his work. His plan was to visit various churches in the area and present his vision for missionary service to the young men who attended. He arrived at his first church on a dark winter's night, only to find that the congregation assembled there was all women. In the entire church, not one male congregant could be seen. Even more troubling for Moffat was that he had prepared a teaching based on Proverbs 8:4, which begins, "Unto you, O men, I call" (KJV). As he scanned the pews, and even the choir loft, his heart despaired. He was certain that God had called him to enlist other young missionaries in this fashion. So where were they? Why had God not delivered? Moffat gave his message anyway, but left the church feeling confused, discouraged, and defeated. What Moffat didn't know, and would only learn later, was that one young man—who had been out of sight, assisting the organist—was deeply moved by the sermon and vowed to follow Moffat in his ministry. When the young man grew up, he honored his vow—he kept his word—and went on to visit the deepest regions of Africa as a missionary. His name was David Livingstone. He also married Moffat's daughter.

Don't you just love how God works?

I have learned a similar lesson. While I was focused on how God was letting me down by not bringing more people into my congregation, I missed the fact that He was using me in various other ways. Because my children's books had made me a rather high-visibility person in southern Oregon, I was asked to visit many different Christian organizations, where I gave my testimony and brought literally thousands of young people to the Lord. I also found, much to my surprise, that the Lord slowly and silently directed my children's books into His corner. Without any influence on my part *at all*, my publishers started asking me to write more Christian-specific titles. Out of these requests emerged some of my favorite books, including *Thank You, God*; *I Know Jesus Loves Me*; and *I Love You, God*.

My suggestion is this: If you're not seeing any fruit in your chosen endeavor, look again. You may have a harvest that you haven't noticed.

4. Tired of Trying

Another reason why people don't finish what they start is they just get "plumb tuckered out," to quote Gabby Hayes, the Western-movie sidekick from the 1940s. Life has a way of doing this to us.

I remember standing and chatting with one of the members of my church congregation several Sundays ago about how life just keeps coming at us; how it is unrelenting in its assault on our quest for peace. It reminded me of the modern-day expression, "going postal," which you may know comes from the sad fact that thirty-five people were killed in almost a dozen post office shootings between 1983 and 1993. Although I can't prove it, I believe the root cause of this phenomenon is the mail itself: It never stops! Imagine what this must feel like. Every day there is a new pile of mail at the post office. Every day you sort it, you file it, you pigeonhole it, and you deliver it. And the next day, there's just as much mail as the day before. It doesn't matter how hard you work. It doesn't matter how smart you are. It doesn't matter if you work late—for free—in an effort to get caught up. The next morning, there will be just as much mail waiting for you—taunting you, laughing at you—as there was the day before. The mail never stops. Until, one day, you can't take it anymore. Or so it seems.

What I shared with my friend after church that day was that you don't have to be a postal worker to "go postal." Instead of the mail coming at you every day, it is life's endless problems. They are unrelenting. They are unceasing. You fix the dryer—the washing machine goes out. You pay your hospital bills—your taxes are due. You finally learn to work the VCR—everything becomes DVD. And it doesn't matter what you do, or how hard you work, or how smart you are, or how late you stay up, the next morning there's always a new mountain of problems waiting for you. It never stops.

Since we're not all postal workers, I like to call the non-postal version of this experience "going primal." One day, when you just can't stand it anymore, you get into a huff and snap at your spouse, curse at a highway worker, refuse to use your hands-free device, or yell at a waitress, until you feel a little better. But then you realize that you've just created a whole batch of new problems that you're now going to have to deal with. And the circus starts all over again.

It should come as no surprise that pastors are not exempt from this type of thing. I call our version "going pastoral," and it is caused by something else that never stops: Sunday. In the ministry, Sunday is always coming at you. A pastor friend of mine calls Sunday "the little dog that keeps nipping at your heels." I agree. It is always out in front of you. It is always waiting for you. It is always looming closer. And it doesn't matter what you do. It doesn't matter how hard you work. It doesn't matter how smart you are. It doesn't matter how late you stay up—next Sunday is always coming! Honestly, the only real peace most pastors feel occurs between lunch on Sunday and breakfast on Monday. Then it starts all over again.

There are other problems, too. Several years back, a survey by Fuller Seminary revealed these somewhat startling findings about pastors:

1. Eighty percent believe that their ministry has had a negative effect on their family.
2. Ninety percent feel they were inadequately trained to meet the needs of the job.
3. Forty percent experience a serious conflict with a church member at least once a month.
4. Seventy percent do not have anyone they consider to be a close friend.[6]

I would like to paraphrase what the apostle Paul writes in 2 Corinthians 11:24-28: "Five times I was given thirty-nine lashes! Three times I was beaten with rods! Once I was even stoned! I've been in danger from rivers, in danger from bandits, and in danger even from my own countrymen! I've been hungry and thirsty, cold and naked! But to top it all off, I've had to take care of the churches!"

That's a pastor for you.

The net result of all this stress may be a pastor who goes "pastoral." This will not be a violent episode, mind you, but it might result in his yelling at the tiny flower girl at a wedding, or refusing to say grace for his breakfast burrito, or just going walkabout some Sunday afternoon.

The gist of the discussion is this: Whether I'm a postal worker, a layperson, or a pastor, when I get really exhausted, I need to do something about it. I need to go wrestle with the Lord.

In the book of Genesis, Jacob is scared to death that his fraternal twin, Esau—who is rapidly bearing down on him with a large army—is about to kill him. Jacob hunkers down in an area he has named Mahanaim (probably meaning "two camps") and waits. The Bible then tells us: "That night Jacob got up and took his two wives, his two female servants and his eleven sons and crossed the ford of the Jabbok. After he had sent them across the stream, he sent over all his possessions." And here it comes, folks: "So Jacob was left alone, and a man wrestled with him till daybreak" (Genesis 32:22–24).

A man wrestled with him till daybreak. Hmm. For those of us who know the story, we have rightly identified this "man" as God Himself. What is so interesting about Jacob's encounter with this preincarnation of Christ is not that he wrestled all night with Him, but that somehow or other Jacob "prevailed." He won the wrestling match! He was victorious! This brings us to a wonderful principle we need to embrace: *Whenever we wrestle with Jesus, to some degree we always prevail.* Always. Though the Bible does not tell us *how* Jacob prevailed, here is what I believe it means. When I am in turmoil, when I am angry and frustrated and ready to explode, if I will go to Jesus in prayer, if I will confess my faults and repent, if I will wrestle with Him all night and say, "Lord, I don't get it! Lord, I'm doing my best! Lord, I'm having trouble with my faith! Lord, why aren't You helping me?" then Jesus will be faithful to let me prevail and to turn my problems into blessings.

If I am "going postal" and shouting, "Lord, the mail never stops!" Jesus will remind me that this is a *good* thing. It gives me job security. It allows me to be part of passing along that important document, of handling that special package, of delivering that much-needed paycheck, or presenting that wonderful Valentine. Then I will say, "Lord, I am so blessed that the mail never stops!" And I have prevailed.

If I am "going primal" and shouting (like Gilda Radner), "Lord, it's always *something*!" Jesus will remind me that this is a *good* thing! I always have a reason to get out of bed in the morning. I always have challenges to help me grow, to help me learn, to help me broaden my abilities, to remind me that I am still in the race, still in the game, still in the ring, still in contention. I'm not just sitting in the dark, gradually turning into a mushroom. Then I will say, "Lord, I am so blessed that it's always something!" And I have just prevailed.

Finally, if I am "going pastoral" and moaning, "O, Lord, another Sunday is coming." Jesus will remind me that this is a *good* thing! I have another opportunity to be filled with His light. I have another chance to stand in His presence. I have another occasion to visit with my Christian brothers and sisters—to sing, pray, worship, and love. I have another chance to listen for God's still, small voice, and another chance to enjoy my favorite two hours of the entire week. Then I will say, "O, Lord, thank You! I am so blessed to always have another Sunday to look forward to!" And I have just prevailed.

After Jacob finished wrestling with the Lord (and prevailed), the Lord gave him a new name, *Israel*, and a new walk—he now limped. His original name, Jacob, was derogatory. It meant "heel snatcher." His parents, Isaac and Rebekah, gave him this name because, during the birth process, he had used his twin brother's heel to pull himself forward, along, and out of the birth canal. He was still holding onto Esau's heel when he emerged into the daylight. In those days, in that culture, a name was intended to reflect a person's character. In the case of Jacob, this turned out to be true. He had spent his entire life using other people to pull himself forward. But after his wrestling match with God, everything changed.

Jacob's new name has two probable meanings: either, "He will rule as God," or, "God fights." Both options work perfectly. When we wrestle with God—when we are not afraid to argue and debate and challenge His decisions in our lives—amazing things start to happen to us. We begin to understand God better. We begin to gain clearer insights into His ways and why He chooses to do what He does. We begin to see the vast power of His love, mercy, patience, and forgiveness. We begin to see how His ways can transform our dark world. All of this makes us better equipped to *rule our lives as God* does. The other interpretation, "God fights," is equally reassuring. When we give our lives to God, when we surrender to His eternal care and provision, when we stand up boldly and tell others about Him, He fights for us! He moves mountains for us. He tames beasts for us. He renders vipers harmless and fire impotent! He goes ahead of us like a swarm of hornets to clear the land for our safe arrival. *God fights*—and I'm glad He does.

We also learn in this story that, during the wrestling match, God touched Jacob's inner thigh, dislocating his hip. That's why Jacob never walked the same way again. This can be true for all of us. I have had a lot wrestling matches with God, and I've learned that this is a very *good* thing to do. God will not be offended, upset, angry, or sullen. He invites us—He *wants* us—to do this. "'Come now, let us settle the matter,' says the LORD" (Isaiah 1:18). This is how our faith grows. In my case, at least, this is also how my Christian "walk" was changed forever. Yours will be too.

There is another aspect to being "tired of trying" that we need to look at. Sometimes the desire to quit comes from feelings of loneliness and isolation. This can be particularly true of people in the creative arts. By necessity, the creative process demands a considerable amount of time spent alone. There is no escaping it. Most artists need to work alone so that people are not leaning over their shoulders, saying things like, "Your character looks like Charlie Brown." What happens, unfortunately, when you've been alone long enough, is that the phone stops ringing, people stop dropping by, e-mails dwindle, your spouse is afraid to bother you, and all human feedback—the type that tells you that you're actually still alive and well—drops off completely. This reminds me of the movie *Papillon,* in which Dustin Hoffman's character, Louis Dega, has been in solitary confinement for so long that, when another prisoner finally is escorted into the cell next to his, all Dega can do is press his face against the small opening in the steel door and ask, "How do I look?"[7] I know the feeling.

There are few endeavors with worse payback than the arts. The term "starving artist" is almost a redundancy. You work and you work and you work, but there is rarely any affirmation that you are an artist at all. After a while, it's easy to start believing you're the only person in the world who struggles like this—especially if you've reached the point where you don't know anyone anymore. This can result in battles with despair and depression and may lead to the desire to just "pack it all in." Don't. You are *not* alone.

There's a great story in 1 Kings about how the prophet Elijah slew 450 prophets of Baal and incurred the wrath of King Ahab and Queen Jezebel, who decided to track him down and kill him. Elijah took off running for his life, but he eventually ran out of gas and stopped in the desert to rest under a broom tree (a large desert bush with only minimal shade). There, Elijah prayed to die. He said, "I have had enough, LORD. . . . Take my life; I am no better than my ancestors" (1 Kings 19:4). What he was saying was, "I have not been any more effective at overcoming your enemies than my ancestors were, Lord." Then he falls asleep.

At this point, an angel nudges Elijah, offers him bread and water and says, "Get up and eat." Elijah accepts the meal, but quickly falls back asleep. Then the angel returns a second time, wakes him up and says, "Get up and eat, for the journey is too much for you" (1 Kings 19:5-7). I love this section of Scripture. We can all reach a point where the journey is too much for us. We can all feel like failures. We can all feel like losers. We can all feel completely lost and alone in our misery. And sometimes we can feel like going to sleep and never waking up. But God understands all this and sends us "angels" to say, "Get up and eat, for the journey is too much for you." Perhaps God's "angel" comes to us in the form of a thought. Perhaps the "angel" comes to us in the form of our spouse. Perhaps the "angel" comes to us in the form of a perfect stranger. Whatever the case, the offering of nourishment and restoration that the "angel" brings to us is always the same: It is bread and water. More specifically, it is the Bread of Life and the Living Water.

The offering that can refresh us is always Jesus Christ Himself.

"Taste and see that the LORD is good" (Psalm 34:8). When I am at my wit's end, when I feel like checking out, when the journey is too much for me, I need to go to the Holy Banquet Table. I need to go to God's Restaurant. I need to go to the Divine Diner where Jesus is served. I need to go to my church—or go to my Bible—and feed my starving and thirsting soul. I need to feast on Jesus. Nothing else will refresh me. Nothing else will give me the strength I need to continue on whatever journey I have begun that has somehow managed to overcome me.

Refreshed, then, Elijah continues his journey.

Eventually, he reaches Mount Horeb (the ancient name for Mount Sinai), also known as "the mountain of the Lord." There, in a cave on the side of the mountain, God's voice comes to him: "What are you doing here, Elijah?" (1 Kings 19:9). What a superb question!

I have used this same question to begin pastors' retreats. I have used this question to launch church services. I have even used this question on myself—many times—to open my own inner dialogue about why I stay in the ministry. "What are you doing here,

P.K.? What are you seeking?" Trying to answer this question can open a floodgate of emotions—and has.

But let us see how Elijah answers this question.

Elijah says, "I have been very zealous for the LORD God Almighty. The Israelites have rejected your covenant, torn down your altars, and put your prophets to death with the sword. I am the only one left, and now they are trying to kill me too" (v. 10). This is a good, solid complaint, but it doesn't answer God's question! The question was: "What are you doing here?"

What follows this exchange is a demonstration of God's power and presence, which I will encourage you to read on your own. For the purposes of this narrative, I need to jump ahead to *after* God's demonstration, when God again asks Elijah, "What are you doing here?" (v. 13). Here is how Elijah answers the question the second time: "I have been very zealous for the LORD God Almighty. The Israelites have rejected your covenant, torn down your altars, and put your prophets to death with the sword. I am the only one left, and now they are trying to kill me, too" (v. 14). This is amazing. Elijah says exactly the same thing he said the first time. To quote former Yankee great Yogi Berra, this is "déjà vu all over again." For whatever reason, Elijah is now clinging to an ironclad alibi about himself for why he failed. A lot of people do this. Rather than examining what they might be doing wrong, or ignoring, or missing—all of which could lead to some painful introspection—many people come up with hair-trigger responses that basically say, when translated properly, "They won't let me." These alibis work every time. It's not their fault. It's out of their hands. It's beyond their control. But here is the pathos of all this: God now says to Elijah, "Yet I reserve seven thousand in Israel—all whose knees have not bowed down to Baal and whose mouths have not kissed him" (v. 18). In other words, "I have seven thousand men just like you right over the next ridge."

Let me see . . . Elijah is running for his life. Elijah wants to quit. Elijah feels completely isolated, abandoned, and alone. Elijah cannot go on because he knows, beyond all certainty, that he is the last of God's servants still alive on this earth. Elijah feels so depressed about this that he is ready to die. But all of it is baloney! Everything he is whining about is not even true! He has created a fantasy about himself simply because he has been out of touch with other people for so long that he has lost track of reality. It reminds me of 1 Corinthians 10:13, which begins, "No temptation has overtaken you except what is common to mankind. And God is faithful; he will not let you be tempted beyond what you can bear." Put another way, nothing is going on in your life that every person doesn't face from time to time. We may *feel* that we have been singled out for extraordinary trials, but we haven't. We've just been alone too long. This is why the Bible urges us not to give up "meeting together, as some are in the habit of doing" (Hebrews 10:25). We need each other to stay strong. We need each other to keep our facts straight. We need each other to feel connected to God.

That said, the key to finding true peace in any endeavor is still to answer this question: "What are you doing here?"

TRY, TRY AGAIN

I need to confess something: I am a big fan of *Dancing with the Stars*. (I know, but I am anyway.) I'm intrigued by how the show unfailingly manages to get to the hearts and souls of its celebrity contestants. Dancing live in front of millions of viewers, these stars have nowhere to hide; any protection they might have felt from their "wall of fame" is swept away in a New York two-step. Confidence dissolves into beads of sweat; bravado collapses into tears. It is oddly refreshing to see the human faces of these socially elevated men and women.

My favorite season to date has been the one that included Bristol Palin. This is not just because she brought some wonderful confusion and apprehension to the show, but because the show's producers decided to give each of the Final Four celebrities—and their corresponding professional dance partners—an opportunity to tell America a little bit about themselves. The five-minute biographical snippets were priceless. One by one, each of the eight finalists discussed the trials, tribulations, setbacks, and achievements that had slowly molded their character to bring them into their current success. The segments included interviews with friends, family, and cowork-ers, who commented on what they had personally witnessed about the "star," or the dancer, regarding their work ethic. As I watched and listened, I noticed the same theme coming up over and over again. It was this: No matter what life had thrown at these people, no matter what physical or emotional shortcom-ings they had to endure or overcome, none of them ever gave up! In fact, it was quite the opposite. When they had setbacks, they tried harder. When they had failures, they pushed through them. When they had weaknesses, they worked around them. When Plan A didn't work, they developed an even better Plan B. And so forth. Comments from family members and friends invariably included observations like these: "She refused to let her problems get her down." "He doesn't know what it means to give up." "She would not stop working at it." "With him, failure was not an option."

What I took away from these brief biographical sketches was that success requires a never-say-die at-titude. Success requires that we "try, try again," no matter what life throws at us. There is a familiar maxim about this truth, which goes: "You cannot fail if you never stop trying."

I was so moved by these testimonies that I sat down and wrote a new children's book, which I titled *Try, Try Again*. My publisher liked the idea, and the book was published in July 2011. On the cover, I drew a little boy sitting on the grass, trying to figure out how to tie the shoelace of one of his red sneakers. His dog, a friendly little Golden Retriever, is sitting next to him, curiously watching this activity. It may be the best cover I have ever done—due to its simplicity. This tiny struggle, which goes on all over the world every day, says it all. Success requires determination. Period.

As I have traveled across this wonderful country of ours, speaking to elementary school students of all ages, races, and colors, I have, on hundreds of occasions, finished my little presentation with my own imitation of Winston Churchill's famous words about never giving up. When I do this, I lean forward on the podium, scrunch up my face, get my voice real gruff and gravelly, and bellow "Never-r-r-r give up! Never! Never! Never! Never! Never-r-r-r!" And each time I say the word *never*, I slam the podium with my hand, making a noise that reverberates off the gymnasium walls. At first, the kids get real wide-eyed— and even a little scared—but then, when they realize that I'm really just a gentle old gasbag, they start cheering, stomping, laughing, and walking around aimlessly. It's wonderful. At one of these schools, I even went to the trouble of creating a cartoon of Winston Churchill, holding his famous cigar, which I made into a transparency so I could project it on the wall while I was thumping the podium. Immediately following the maiden voyage of this new approach, a teacher came up to me and read me the riot act! She was absolutely livid. She was scandalized that I would show someone holding a cigar to these very young and impressionable students. Didn't I know that I was encouraging smoking? I won't tell you what I was thinking during her tirade, but I put the transparency away and never used it again.

It took me thirty years to realize that I had been misquoting Churchill at schools all across America. What he actually said at Harrow School on October 29, 1941, after England had survived massive bombings by the German Luftwaffe, was this:

> For everyone, surely, what we have gone through in this period—I am addressing myself to the School—surely from this period of ten months this is the lesson: Never give in! Never give in! Never, never, never, never—in nothing, great or small, large or petty—never give in, except to convictions of honor and good sense! Never yield to force! Never yield to the apparently overwhelming might of the enemy!

Great speech. Great advice. By the way, I don't think kids should smoke cigars either.

ONE MORE STEP

When I was in my thirties, I had a drinking problem. It was so bad, in fact, that at one point I did not expect to live past my thirty-seventh birthday. Fortunately, I rallied and I have now been sober for twenty-seven years. But I will never forget how hard it was to quit drinking. All my friends were drunks, so there was a social aspect of my recovery that I needed to overcome. My friends started treating me like a pariah at their parties. So I stopped going to their parties. There was also a mild physical withdrawal to cope with, but that was relatively easy for me. On the other hand, the psychological aspects of getting "clean and sober" were hideously difficult. Like many alcoholics, I did not believe I was an alcoholic. In fact, like virtually every nonrecovering alcoholic I have ever known, I chose to cling to the popular self-delusion that "I just like to drink." My inability to get to the truth about myself—often called *denial*—went on for months. One day, however, I was sitting in the bathtub, really wrangling with whether or not I was an alcoholic, when it hit me like a thunderbolt: *Nonalcoholics don't think this way.* They don't spend every single moment of every single day thinking about alcohol! I got up out of the tub, exuberant, because I had finally acknowledged and accepted the truth: I was an alcoholic! I wish I could tell you that this made things easier for me, but it did not. For months, I continued to whine and bemoan my great loss—drinking—to my wife. Finally, God bless her, she said, "Do whatever you want." That was the real beginning of my recovery. What she had done, in one brief sentence, was to hand my problem back to me. She made me take ownership of it, and suddenly everything changed.

That's when I started living "one step at a time."

Many problems, or challenges, in life are like this. We look at the big picture, the whole picture, and the solution seems too vast to manage. But when we break the problem into its smaller components, it becomes workable. A friend of mine likes to say, "Just do what you know and you'll know what to do." Amen. I may not be able to run a marathon right now, but I can run a mile. I may not be able to build a patio, but I know how to buy wood. And I may not be able to quit drinking for the rest of my life, but I can skip drinking today.

In 1945, while living in East Prussia, Aleksandr Solzhenitsyn was arrested by the Soviet police for writing disparaging comments about Joseph Stalin in letters to friends. He was accused of "founding a hostile organization," and on July 1, 1945, he was sentenced to eight years of hard labor in a notoriously cruel Soviet gulag.

And the misery began.

Endless days of slow starvation and backbreaking work became his life. One bleak day followed another. One violent beating followed another. One empty meal followed another. His life became a perpetual cycle of torture, deprivation, and hopelessness. Then one day, the sheer weight of this was too much for him. Right in the middle of some pointless—and endless—digging he was being forced to do, Solzhenitsyn dropped his shovel to the ground and sat down on a nearby bench, resolving never to get up again. He knew, and accepted, the penalty for this: He would surely be beaten to death with his own shovel. It was a common occurrence there.

As he sat waiting to die, he noticed an old man, sitting on the same bench, about two feet away from him. He was slumped forward, staring blankly into the dirt, and his face held the lifeless expression of so many of the gulag's condemned prisoners—one of defeat, surrender, and acceptance. But suddenly, the old man took a stick and began drawing something in the dirt at Solzhenitsyn's feet. As Solzhenitsyn watched in silence, the man slowly and methodically traced out the image of a simple cross. It was the cross of Christ. In the next few moments, as Solzhenitsyn contemplated the significance—and the power—of this message from the old man, he made a decision that not only changed his life but eventually changed the world. He wearily stood up and went back to work—one more time.

Years later, his writings exposed the brutality and failure of Communism as a social system, and in 1970, he won the Nobel Prize for Literature. Finally, on June 5, 2007, Russian president Vladimir Putin awarded Solzhenitsyn the prestigious State Prize of the Russian Federation for his humanitarian work.

All because he stood up one more time.

Perseverance is often the key to success. We may need to stand up one more time. We may need to take one more step. We may need to fight one more battle. We may need to stay sober one more day. My friend who made himself a millionaire twice over liked to say, "Success in business comes from doing a lot of *little* things right." I agree. In life, as well as in business, it's often the little things that make the biggest difference.

Because I'm a writer—and teach writing—I like to collect scraps of information about how other writers had to struggle before they became successful. Here is a short list of some writers who did not give up, did not give in, did not surrender; who moved in to stay, who finished what they started, who stood up one more time—and who took one more step: Richard Hooker, who wrote *M*A*S*H*, was rejected by twenty-one publishers before he took *one more step* and sold his manuscript to William Morrow; Thor Heyerdahl, author of *Kon Tiki*—one of the most extraordinary raft voyages ever recorded—was turned down by twenty publishers until he took *one more step* and found himself at Rand McNally; Richard Bach, who penned *Jonathan Livingston Seagull*, was rejected by eighteen publishers before he took *one more step* and arrived at MacMillan; Patrick Dennis, who wrote *Auntie Mame*, was turned away by seventeen publishers, until *one more step* brought him to Vanguard Publishing; and Theodore Geisel, better known as Dr. Seuss, wrote his first book, *And to Think I Saw It on Mulberry Street*, only to see it rejected by twenty-three publishers. Fortunately, he also took *one more step* and found Vantage Press.

Now, let's just imagine what would have happened if Dr. Seuss had stopped moving forward toward his dream: We might never have had *Green Eggs and Ham*.

John Calvin Coolidge Jr., thirtieth president of the United States (1923–1929), was also known as Silent Cal, because he rarely had anything to say. I find it interesting, then, that Silent Cal could come up with anything as marvelously articulate and profound as the following advice: "Press on. Nothing in the world can take the place of persistence. Talent will not; nothing is more common than unrewarded talent. Education alone will not; the world is full of educated failures. Persistence alone is omnipotent."

Persistence alone is omnipotent.

It Is Finished

We began this Third Step to Making a Difference with Jesus kneeling in the garden of Gethsemane, asking His Father to remove the specter of crucifixion from His future. He said, "Abba, Father, . . . everything is possible for you. Take this cup from me . . ." (Mark 14:36).

I purposely did not finish this verse, in order to make a point. Suppose Jesus had decided *not* to finish what He started. Suppose Jesus had decided *not* to take that one more step. Where would we be? Where would the world be? I have always appreciated how nineteenth-century British historian William Lecky described Jesus' impact on us and on the world. He writes: "It was reserved for Christianity to present to the world an ideal character, which through all the changes of the eighteen centuries has inspired the hearts of men with an impassioned love, has shown itself capable of acting on all ages, nations, tempera-ments, and conditions, has been not only the high-est pattern of virtue but the strongest incentive to its practice. . . . The simple record of three short years of active life [of Jesus' ministry] has done more to regenerate and to soften mankind than all the dis-quisitions of philosophers and all the exhortations of moralists."[8]

How wonderful for us that Jesus did not leave His prayer in Gethsemane unfinished, but quickly added, "Yet not what I will, but what you will," and went on to finish what He started.

Jesus always knew the answer to the question: "What are you doing here?"

When the Jewish leaders sought to kill Jesus for "making himself equal with God" (John 5:18), He re-sponded to them, using the legal practice of the time, which required witnesses to attest to His claims. Jesus said, "I have testimony weightier than that of John [the Baptist]. For the works that the Father has given me to *finish*—the very works that I am doing—testify that the Father has sent me" (John 5:36, emphasis added).

After the Samaritan woman at Jacob's Well had run back to her village to tell others about Jesus be-ing the Messiah, the disciples encouraged Jesus to eat some of the food they had just purchased. Jesus re-sponded by saying, "My food . . . is to do the will of him who sent me and to *finish* his work" (John 4:34, emphasis added).

Then, in the sixth hour on the cross at Calvary, with the dark sky looming menacingly above, Jesus, when He had received the vinegar, said, "'It is *finished.*' With that, he bowed his head and gave up his spirit" (John 19:30, emphasis added).

This pattern is clear. The greatest man who ever lived believed in doing what He said He was going to do—and in finishing what He started.

Should we do less?

STEP ONE:
WORK HARD

STEP TWO:
GO IN THE STRENGTH
YOU HAVE

STEP THREE:
FINISH WHAT YOU START

Be Patient

*Success always comes when preparation
meets opportunity.*
Henry Hartman

Today, many scholars believe that the book of Job is actually the oldest book in the Bible, preceding even the book of Genesis in terms of authorship. If this is so, and the underlying theme of the story is *patience*—as in "the patience of Job"—then patience becomes a founding principle of God's Word to us. He wants us to understand, accept, and apply godly patience in our lives. God did not test Job, but God allowed Satan to test Job severely. God occasionally allows Satan to test us severely, too. This is because without a test, we have no *testi*mony. As difficult as this may be for us to grasp at times, God uses us to reveal Himself to the lost souls of this world. But the only way He can be seen is through different forms of contrast: kindness in the face of hatred, mercy in response to evil, forgiveness in place of retaliation . . . or through any godly behavior that contradicts normal human behavior and baffles the nonbelieving observer. This is when God's light shines the brightest in Satan's darkness, which is the greatest *contrast* of them all. Patience under fire is a classic example. In the Sermon on the Mount (Luke 6:27–38), Jesus offers His disciples the following guidelines for demonstrating the types of behavior that reveal the truth of God's existence:

> Love your enemies.
> Do good to those who hate you.
> Be a blessing to those who curse you.
> Pray for those who mistreat you.
> Do not retaliate.
> Give freely.
> Treat others the way you want to be treated.

I know an elderly Christian woman who went into the hospital for back surgery and ended up losing the use of her left leg. Instead of throwing a fit and threatening to sue everyone involved, this woman chose to believe that God had allowed this "test" in order to give her an opportunity to reveal Him to others. And she did. When I visited her hospital room to pray with her, I found her surrounded by patients, nurses, doctors, technicians, and others who were laughing, smiling, and generally basking in the joy God was radiating through her. Seven years later, she still has not regained the use of her left leg, but she is as upbeat as ever. She is confidently and patiently awaiting a miracle. And she is still radiating God's joy.

ON THE SHELF

The phone rang. It was Rosemary, Bud Thompson's secretary. "Mr. Thompson needs to see you in his office," she said. She should have added, "And bring your playbook." Even though I had been expecting the call, I could still feel a shock wave of apprehension go through me. I stood up, looked around my small office, and then headed down the hallway to Bud's office. It was a short trip. Rosemary was sitting at her desk outside the office, and she looked up at me with sympathetic eyes. Bud, who was on the phone, waved me in with a forced smile. There was no longer any doubt in my mind. To quote Marlon Brando in *On the Waterfront*, I was about to get "a one-way ticket to Palookaville."[9]

The company I worked for was located in San Diego and manufactured products we called "uninterruptible power systems." These ecru-colored tin boxes came in all sizes—from toaster small to refrigerator large—and were essentially sophisticated bundles of batteries designed to keep computers running if the primary source of electricity failed. Under the leadership of our founder and president, Ken Olson, we had been very successful. Too successful, I guess. In 1985, a huge company in Chicago that had been following our story for a couple of years decided to purchase us. Although they assured us that no jobs would be lost, they were just kidding. Slowly but surely, one by one, most of the middle managers were led away from their offices, never to be seen again. It was all very Mafioso: "Hey, it's just business, Frankie."

Even though I had seen plenty of others take the "walk of shame," my hopes still sprang eternal. I was the director of marketing communications and considered myself the creative genius of the company—an opinion that I alone held and supported. In any case, I knew my time was near the day Ken Olson himself got the ax and was replaced by the director of engineering. I called Ken at his home that evening and offered to help him any way I could, and he seemed both touched and grateful. I got the ax exactly one week later—this, after twelve long years of sort-of loyal service.

I would like to say I took it well, but I did not. Although we often hear about, and read about, people losing their jobs, we rarely think much about it. It's just life. But when it happens to us, personally, it is a whole different ball game. Many of us go into shock. Many go into deep depression. Many go around asking total strangers, "Are you my mother?" And so forth. It can be very tough. To the credit of the company that bought us, they did provide a sort of post-hatchet counseling service for all the terminated employees. We were encouraged to attend a series of free job-skills training sessions, where we could identify and locate new jobs we might be good at. Unfortunately, most of us had just *lost* the jobs we were good at, so the sessions seemed empty and gratuitous. I found myself sitting across the desk from a counselor, staring blankly back at her and feeling very much like Aleksandr Solzhenitsyn on the gulag bench: half dead and hopeless.

Remember, though, as I mentioned in Step One, one of my life slogans is *the other side of disaster is always opportunity*. Always. Two weeks later, I got a telephone call from ex-president Ken. He said, "Let's get together. There's something I want to talk to you about."

In a nutshell, Ken—a fan of the five children's books I had published at that time—offered to bankroll me for a year in order to help me launch a full-time writing and illustrating career. This was my first encounter with famed artist Henry Hartman's maxim: Success always comes when preparation meets opportunity. Frankly, I was *prepared*. Even though my children's books were few in number, I knew what I was doing and I knew how to do it. The *opportunity* that presented itself I could never have anticipated. But when these two elements finally *met*, it was "Game, set, and match, Mr. Hallinan." My children's book career took off like a rocket, and I have never been able to thank Ken Olson enough.

One of my first manuscripts out of the chute was a sweet little number I created simply to tell my two sons, Kenny and Mike, that I loved them. I put both of them into the book—as cartoon characters, of course—and when I finished writing and illustrating the manuscript, I sent it off to every publisher I could think of. No one was interested.

Beginning writers sometimes assume that publishers will give them reasons for rejecting a manuscript. But this is rarely true. Most manuscripts come back with an unsigned form letter that reads,

"Unfortunately, your manuscript does not match our publishing needs at this time." I don't blame them. I have received a lot of unsolicited manuscripts over the years. Most authors want to know if their book ideas are great or just really good—and often I wish I had a form letter to send back to them. Frankly, I have long believed that I spend more time agonizing over how to say nice things about the manuscripts than the authors spent writing them. Anyway, only one publisher sent me a comment for improving my manuscript about my love for my two sons. I was told that having two characters on the page made the narrator's point of view confusing. In other words, I had written the text in the literary first-person omniscient, and the publisher thought it was unclear who was speaking to whom. I made a mental note of this and sent it back out again. Finally, however, I put the manuscript up on a shelf in my studio and focused my energies on other new book concepts.

Two years later, I had my second encounter with preparation and opportunity meeting.

I was in my studio, doing nothing in particular that I remember, when my telephone rang. It was a female editor from a publisher that I had worked with on a few occasions. After some social amenities, she got to the point: "Do you have any unpublished manuscripts lying around that you could send us?" She explained that they simply did not have enough new books for their spring catalog. I told her I had one book that no one had been interested in—the one about my two sons—but I would be happy to send it to her. She said she was very interested and, yes, to please send it as soon as possible.

The rest is history.

I changed the illustrations in the manuscript to feature only one character instead of two and sent it in. *How Do I Love You?* was soon published and went on to become my best-selling book ever, now nearing the two-million-copies-sold mark. It was simply a matter of preparation and opportunity crossing.

This could be you.

Perhaps you are fully prepared for success, but there has been no substantial opportunity. Or perhaps a good opportunity has come your way, but you were not fully prepared. Be patient. It's only a matter of time. In a writer's life, the best approach to success is always to keep going—no matter what. If you're stuck on a word, keep writing anyway. If you hate what you're writing, keep writing anyway. If you feel like tearing up your entire manuscript, keep writing anyway. If you stop—if you don't keep writing—ten years will pass, and you will still be working on chapter one. Finally, once you've finished and sent off your manuscript, don't just sit around hoping and praying that some publisher will like it. Immediately start working on your next book.

This principle works no matter what your chosen endeavor might be. Don't take your foot off the gas pedal and coast. This will only delay your arrival that much longer.

In the Storm

That day when evening came, he said to his disciples, "Let us go over to the other side." Leaving the crowd behind, they took him along, just as he was, in the boat. There were also other boats with him. A furious squall came up, and the waves broke over the boat, so that it was nearly swamped. Jesus was in the stern, sleeping on a cushion. The disciples woke him and said to him, "Teacher, don't you care if we drown?"

He got up, rebuked the wind and said to the waves, "Quiet! Be still!" Then the wind died down and it was completely calm.

He said to his disciples, "Why are you so afraid? Do you still have no faith?"

They were terrified and asked each other, "Who is this? Even the wind and the waves obey him!"

They went across the lake to the region of the Gerasenes. (Mark 4:35–5:1)

Life is a storm.

Sometimes we feel as if we spend our entire lives sailing in and out of storms. But just the opposite is true. We *live* in a storm and spend our lives sailing in and out of the eye. That's because we inhabit a fallen world where chaos is the norm and calm is the exception. Patience can be difficult to maintain when we are in constant fear of drowning.

There are several wonderful lessons in this story, however, that should bring comfort to all of us.

Jesus and His disciples are in a tiny ship on the Sea of Galilee. Suddenly a furious storm howls in and threatens to sink them. Mark describes this tumult as a "great storm of wind." The Greek word he uses for "great" is *megas,* the same word from which we get our English words megahit, megastar, mega-mucho, and the like: It means *the maximum, utmost, and greatest possible.* So this mega-storm—this *maximum* storm— slams into the tiny ship, swamping it with water and driving the disciples into an understandable panic. They race to the back of the boat, where Jesus is sleeping on a pillow, and wake Him up.

"Teacher," they shout, "don't you care if we drown?" At this point, Jesus gets up, rebukes the wind, and says to the storm, "Shush, be muzzled!" Mark tells us that the wind ceased and there was "a great calm." Now Jesus turns to His disciples and asks them, "Why are you so afraid? Do you still have no faith?"

There is more to this story, but I will save it for later. Right now, I want us to focus on a few important insights. First, while we are patiently waiting to cross any calm sea, invariably we will—at some point—sail back into the storm. There's no avoiding it. But if we have accepted Jesus as our Lord and Savior, then He is in our ship with us, and He is unsinkable. This makes us unsinkable too! Second, although we've all heard stories about the struggle between good and evil— between God and Satan—there really is no struggle at all. Jesus mildly commands the evil minions of the storm to "be quiet," and they slink off like junkyard dogs. Third, Jesus asks the disciples, "How is it that you still have no faith?" He asks this because He is grieved at how little they have learned about Him in the time they've been together. The disciples seem strangely ignorant of His power and glory. Even this early in His ministry, Jesus had already taught in the synagogue, and the people were "amazed at his teaching" (Mark 1:22). He had already healed a demon-possessed man (vv. 23–26), and had healed Peter's mother-in-law of a fever (vv. 29–31). He also healed a multitude of sick and possessed people who came to Peter's door (vv. 32–34). He had healed a leper (v. 40) and a man stricken with palsy (2:5).

And yet the disciples who have witnessed all these things remain "iffy" about their faith. Jesus asks them, "How is this possible?"

He asks me the same thing.

Jesus has demonstrated His love, His mercy, His power, and His grace to me so many times that I am ashamed to admit that, on occasion, my faith still fails me. I'm embarrassed at how often I've asked Jesus, "Lord, don't You care that I'm perishing? Don't You care that my ship is sinking?" And I'm sad that I don't have greater *patience* in the storm. I just want it to be over.

My final observation about this story is that Mark says the ensuing calm was "great." Again he uses the Greek word *megas*. In other words, with one simple command, Jesus turned the worst possible storm into the best possible calm. When I take a long, hard, and honest look back at all the tests, trials, tribulations, and storms in my life, I see that Jesus has always done this for me. He has always turned my clouds into rainbows.

He did this for Job, too.

At the end of Job's painful period of waiting for God to get Satan off his back, the Bible tells us: "The LORD restored his fortunes and gave him twice as much as he had before. . . . He had fourteen thousand sheep, six thousand camels, a thousand yoke of oxen and a thousand donkeys. And he also had seven sons and three daughters. . . . Job lived a hundred and forty years; he saw his children and their children to the fourth generation. And so Job died, an old man and full of years" (Job 42:10–17).

Of all the personality traits Christians should have, the one that is hardest to find, but that God rewards the most, is patience. God doubled Job's possessions. God filled Job's life with goodness and splendor. God increased Job's property and extended the years of his life. God rewarded Job with beautiful daughters and a whole passel of grandchildren. God thanked Job for his steadfast faithfulness. He will thank us, too.

In the Fullness of Time

I have a fraternal twin brother named Mike. He looks nothing like me. I was born seven minutes ahead of him, back in 1944, but it might as well have been seven years. By the time we were in eighth grade, I was really fat and he was really skinny. Not only were we physical opposites, but our parents had named us Pat and Mike. This, of course, reminded people of the poem that goes, "Pat and Mike look alike!" As Mike said years later, "We were a walking setup for a joke." It was true. The other kids would look at us and shout, "How can you guys be twins? You don't even *look* alike!" Today, Mike lives in Laguna Beach, California, where he works as a fine artist. He uses acrylics to create truly beautiful paintings, mostly of seascapes, beach scenes, abandoned trucks, and Mexican gas stations. In a business where no one succeeds, he has done extremely well. I once asked him how famous he was. He replied, "I'm as famous as someone can be who hasn't been plucked out of the pot." I know what he means. He means that you can spend your entire life doing wonderful work, but unless you are "plucked out of the pot"—by Oprah Winfrey, or some such person—your career may never soar to the heights that others in your field have reached.

Back in 1971, Mike was approached by an artist's agent who asked him to submit some paintings so that he could be considered for the honor of "official artist" for the 1972 Olympics in Munich. This was one of those rare opportunities to be "plucked out of the pot." And he pursued it. The gig eventually went to LeRoy Neiman, but Mike just shrugged it off. "Most things don't happen," he said matter-of-factly, meaning that most great promises of instant fame rarely come to anything. This has been my observation as well. There are rarely any quick jumps, catapults, or shortcuts in a career—which is another reason why patience is so important. Without patience, every artist I know would be even crazier than they already are.

I used to tell people that I didn't care about getting rich—only about becoming famous. I got my wish. Today, I'm not rich, but I am *mildly* famous. In fact, a publicist I worked with once said, "P.K., you're the most famous person in America that nobody has ever heard of." I laughed. I still laugh about it. This truth has become a prime example of being careful what you wish for.

The Bible says, "When the set time had fully come, God sent his Son, born of a woman, born under the law, to redeem those under law, that we might receive adoption to sonship" (Galatians 4:4–5). To me, this is the key to becoming more patient. We need to consider and understand God's "fullness-of-time" architecture. The following question and answer tells us how this works:

> **Q:** When did God send His only begotten Son into the world to save humankind?
> **A:** When the set time had fully come; when everything was in perfect readiness; when doing so could achieve maximum results.

This is how God always decides *when* something should be done.

Even though it may not be obvious that God has a perfect plan for each of our lives, He does. These plans are the basis for His timing and for His divine interventions. The Bible tells us: "The Lord is . . . not willing that any should perish but that all should come to repentance" (2 Peter 3:9 NKJV). The Greek word for "all" here is *pas*. It means *all*. Because God wants *everyone* to receive the gift of eternal life—and none to be lost—He structures the events of humanity and history to facilitate this.

A good example of this can be found in the story of Joseph in the book of Genesis. After spending several years in slavery—and in prison—Joseph was elevated by Pharaoh to the office of prime minister of Egypt, the second most powerful position in the land. This was due to Joseph's dream that predicted a terrible famine engulfing the entire country. Pharaoh responded by having every silo in the land stuffed to the top with grain, thereby saving millions of lives. Pharaoh thanked Joseph by giving him a distinguished and powerful job. Joseph's brothers, on the other hand, who had sold Joseph into slavery years earlier, now must come to him, trembling and asking for mercy. Here, Joseph delivers one of my favorite lines in the entire Bible: "You intended to harm me, but God intended it for good to accomplish what is now being done, the saving of many lives" (Genesis 50:20). There it is. This is always why God does *what* He does *when* He does it: *to save people's lives.*

When I fervently pray, asking God to change some condition in my life, and nothing happens, it's because God knows that leaving me in my current situation or condition, and waiting until a future time—for the *fullness of time*—will result in *saving many lives.* This is where our godly patience can come from—knowing that God's timing is perfect and that He always uses us, or our predicaments, for the greater good of humanity.

God says, "My thoughts are not your thoughts, neither are your ways my ways. . . . As the heavens are higher than the earth, so are my ways higher than your ways and my thoughts than your thoughts" (Isaiah 55:8–9). I like what someone said about these verses: "Any God small enough for me to understand would not be big enough for me to worship." Amen.

Waiting on Straight Street

In any endeavor, there is always a period of waiting between the launch and the landing. Earlier, we talked about Saul of Tarsus and his collision with Jesus on the road to Damascus. Saul, blinded and in utter confusion, said, "Lord, what would you have me do?" Jesus answered, "Get up and go into the city, and you will be told what you must do" (Acts 9:6). Saul's companions then led him by the hand into the city of Damascus and deposited him in a house on a road called Straight Street. There he sat, in total darkness, for the next three days, not having a clue why he was sitting there—or what was going on—or if he would ever be able to see again.

In the meantime, Jesus was busy preparing a person, a disciple named Ananias, to go to Saul. Ananias, however, was balking because of all the terrible things he had heard about Saul and the way Saul relished persecuting, torturing, and even murdering Christians. No doubt the magnitude of Ananias's fears and complaints were extending the time that Saul had to sit in darkness. But Jesus patiently explained to Ananias why it was important to go to Saul, and three days later Ananias arrived at the house on Straight Street, touched Saul, and Saul's sight was immediately restored (see Acts 9:7–17).

This story could apply to any of us.

The parallels between Saul's experience and our entering into any new career endeavor are many. First, there is the inevitable collision between the old you and the new you—or perhaps between you and God—which may knock you off your feet, so to speak. Adjusting to new ideas, new ways, new schedules, new demands—and a whole new lifestyle—can be unsettling. You may feel wobbly, uncertain of your footing, and off balance. But this never lasts long. Second, there is always a period of blind waiting. You may not notice any movement or progress or impact from your early efforts. But you can take comfort in knowing that somewhere someone is being prepared by God to come to you, whether by phone, by mail, by e-mail, or in person. When this happens, you will start to *see* again. Your path will become clearer; your plans will become more crystallized. Along this same line, you can also be certain that there are already events occurring—beyond your vision—that are designed specifically to benefit your future. Third, you have been deposited on Straight Street. This is no mistake.

In Scripture, the concept of being "straightened" means to be made morally and spiritually stronger so that you are prepared to walk the "straight and narrow" path. In business, this can mean the same thing, but it can also mean to "perfect your skills" for the tasks you have chosen. "Waiting on Straight Street," then, is a certain length of time that must be given over to the preparing of ourselves for our success, as preordained by God.

I mentioned earlier that I spent twenty years in corporate America before I was able to become a full-time children's author. For me, this was a period of "waiting on Straight Street." It was a time in my life when my skills were being sharpened and expanded so that I would be ready for the next phase of my career. During this period of my life, I learned about graphic design. I learned about type fonts. I learned about preparing and pasting up layouts. I learned advertising and publicity. I even learned about business. But most important—although I had been dazzling people for years with my writing skills—I finally learned about *real* writing, like how to punctuate and that sort of thing. Oddly, it was Ken Olson who taught me the true craft of writing. I say "oddly," because his degree was in electrical engineering, and electrical engineers are not exactly celebrated for their writing prowess. In fact, just the opposite. One of my primary jobs at Ken's company was to translate engineering babble into English. But Ken himself, for whatever reason, knew *everything* there was to know about writing, and he routinely beat me to death with my mistakes in our manuals, catalogs, and annual reports. Often, I felt like I was working in a gulag; but I've never been able to thank him enough for helping me become a real writer.

In the ministry, I've also had times of "waiting on Straight Street." Though I've told many people that I went into the ministry for all the wrong reasons—to be the center of attention, entertainer of the year, beloved windbag, and all that—I now believe this is not true. The desperation and despair I suffered after stepping down from my first church could only have come from a feeling of rejecting God's supernatural calling. In other words, I had very little to do with my own going into the ministry. All I said was yes. Fifteen years later, I continue to rejoice that "God's gifts and his call are irrevocable" (Romans 11:29). This means He will never withdraw His calling on my life—even when I act like a complete imbecile.

In some ways, we never really get off of "Straight Street." The good Lord is always preparing some reluctant "Ananias" to come to us. He is always stirring up events and opportunities beyond our knowledge that will affect our lives. And we are never completely "straightened" for the road ahead. As a children's author, I will always be struggling to perfect my craft. As a minister, I will always be struggling to perfect my heart. Both take a lot of patience and a lot of time in the dark.

When Is Enough, Enough?

In business, ministry, or just in life, impatience can lead us to compare ourselves to others. But we cannot assess our progress by staring at someone else's accomplishments. In fact, we can't even assess *their* progress by staring at their accomplishments. I remember when my friend Spencer Johnson made national inroads with his book *The One-Minute Manager.* He was pleased, of course, but he said something I have never forgotten. He said, "P.K., you will know you've finally made it when you start getting sued." There is a lot of truth to this. Whenever we envy someone, we need to remember that we do not have a clue what that person is really going through.

There are, of course, all kinds of things that can go wrong in a business endeavor. I remember once reading a mailing I received, titled "Rotten Rejections."[10] It highlighted a number of rejection letters sent to some of the world's most famous authors—before their books became classics. Here are just three:

> "Regret the American public is not interested in anything on China." (Pearl S. Buck, *The Good Earth*)

> "The girl does not, it seems to me, have a special feeling or perception that would lift the book above the 'curiosity' level." (*The Diary of Anne Frank*)

"These stories have trees in them." (Norman McLean, *A River Runs Through It*)

Although these rejections were anomalies—even comical—rejection in any business is a fact of life. But how much is enough? It is difficult to say.

Moses spent forty years in the desert, leading 2.5 million surly Israelites from one broom tree to another. As he did this, he was confidently expecting eventually to take them into the Promised Land. This, however, was not to be. It turned out that God entrusted Joshua with this honor. So Moses died near the banks of the Jordan River, never getting his chance to cross over with everybody into Canaan. This reminds me again of the movie *On the Waterfront*, where Marlon Brando's prize-fighting character, Terry Malloy, finally lands an important boxing match, only to hear, "Kid, this ain't your night."

This ain't your night.

A similar fate befell King David. The Bible tells us that David was "a man after [God's] own heart" (see 1 Samuel 13:14). Yet, as dear to God's heart as David was, David's greatest desire—to build a permanent temple for the Lord—was not to be. Instead, God gave this honor to David's son Solomon.

Then there's Peter. After responding three times to Jesus' question, "Do you love me?" Peter listens as Jesus describes Peter's future crucifixion. "When you were younger you dressed yourself and went where you wanted; but when you are old you will stretch out your hands, and someone else will dress you and lead you where you do not want to go" (John 21:18). Peter then, naturally enough, wants to know how his pal John is going to die. Jesus replies: "If I want him to remain alive until I return, what is that to you? You must follow me" (v. 22). In other words, "It's none of your business what John is going to do. Keep your eyes on Me."

In a nutshell, God has different plans for each one of us. This means we might be doing everything well, but still be outside of God's perfect will for our lives—and experiencing "rotten rejections."

There is, of course, the opposite side to this. We may be doing everything well—and be in the exact, perfect center of God's will—and still be experiencing "rotten rejections." Why? Because serving God means fighting Satan.

There is a joke that goes as follows:

> **Man:** Why should I repent? The devil isn't bothering me.
> **Friend:** That's because you're both going the same direction.

If I am following Jesus, I am experiencing resistance; there is no avoiding this. When I first became a Christian, I thought all the "persecution" stuff I'd heard about was a bunch of hooey—and I was determined not to become one of God's "suffering servants." But I quickly found out that this is impossible. To put it bluntly, the unbelieving world *hates* God. These folks don't necessarily know they hate Him, by the way, they just do. Jesus says, "They hated me without reason" (John 15:25). Jesus also says, "Everyone will hate you because of me" (Luke 21:17). An irrefutable tenet of God's universe is that darkness hates light, evil hates good, and nonbelievers hate believers. There can be no communion between polar opposites. It is both ironic and sad that, while this nation firmly believes it is becoming increasingly *enlightened*, it is, in fact, becoming increasingly *darkened*. No matter where we live, the rats have already slipped through the cracks, the night artists have already blemished the view, and the day thieves have already hacked into the bank accounts. Sooner or later, the darkness always arrives. Without God, there is no stopping it.

I have paid a price for choosing the light. We all do. Sarah Palin recently said to her daughter Bristol, "There are a lot of haters out there." It's a good observation and the right word: "haters." I became aware of this very early on in my Christian walk. Back in 1995, the then-publisher of our local newspaper—a fellow Christian—invited me to write a regular weekly column for the religion section. I guess he figured that a combination of kiddy-book author and small-church pastor was irresistible. I guess I figured that, too. In any case, I happily agreed and I began churning out a small Friday offering called "In the Word." My premise was to choose a section of Scripture and expound on its application to our lives. I was not prepared for the hate mail that followed. Not only did a rash of angry letters pour into my mailbox, but my public exposure as "one of those born-again nutcases" took its toll in other avenues of my life. Some bookstores stopped carrying my books. Some schools stopped inviting me for assemblies, fearing I might be too much of a risk for violating the separation of church and state. Other people just quietly stopped doing business with me.

Kid, this ain't your night.

I continued writing the column anyway—for about a year—until the publisher found a better job, and the paper sought out a new, "more flexible" Christian minister—one who wouldn't harp on all that Jesus stuff. They had plenty of those to choose from.

My point is this: We may face a lot of "rotten rejections" for nothing that we have done wrong. Often, we're rejected for what we're doing right.

That said, at some point we may need to take a hard look at the fruit we're bearing—or not bearing—and ask ourselves some difficult questions, such as: When is enough, enough? Is it time to throw in the towel? Should I try something else? Do I need to move on?

Before I answer this, let me say that I have learned in my years as a Christian that one of my spiritual gifts is that of *encouragement*. I'm a born cheerleader. If you've done something good, I'm likely the first person to run up to you and say so. I can't help myself. God has seen to it that this gift burns inside me like

Nebuchadnezzar's fiery furnace—seven times hotter than it needs to be. So the idea of suggesting "quitting" to anyone is against my nature. With that in mind, I have a suggestion for you to consider.

A young pastor approached me at a pastors' retreat and questioned me on this exact subject. He had planted a tiny church in a remote community in the forests of Northern California, and two years later his church had grown from dismal to nonexistent. "How long do you think I should keep going?" he asked.

Have you ever noticed that God sometimes sends you the exact Scripture you need when you need it most? He does this to help us answer the question the way He wants it answered. Here is the verse that God sent to me to give to the struggling young pastor:

"When you enter the land and plant any kind of fruit tree, regard its fruit as forbidden. For three years you are to consider it forbidden; it must not be eaten. In the fourth year all its fruit will be holy, an offering of praise to the LORD. But in the fifth year you may eat of its fruit. In this way your harvest will be increased" (Leviticus 19:23–25).

Paraphrasing this, I think it's reasonable to say, "If you follow these steps, your harvest will be increased in the fifth year." And that's exactly what I told him. "Give it five years."

GETTING TO THE OTHER SIDE

Earlier, we took a look at Jesus and the disciples trying to cross the Sea of Galilee in a furious storm.

Jesus calmed the storm with a simple, "Peace, be still!" (Mark 4:39 NKJV). Then we looked at how Jesus confronted the disciples about their lack of faith, especially when these men had seen Jesus perform many previous miracles. He said, "How is it that you have no faith?" The Bible adds, "And they feared exceedingly, and said to one another, 'Who can this be, that even the wind and the sea obey Him!'" (Mark 4:40-41 NKJV). Then the next chapter begins, "Then they came to the other side of the sea, into the country of the Gadarenes" (Mark 5:1 NKJV).

The disciples "feared exceedingly"—even though they had already seen Jesus perform many miracles. How can this be? It "can be" because miracles have never convinced anybody of anything. I was watching a television show one evening that featured a world-famous magician and his lovely assistant. At one point, the assistant—who was standing beside the magician—dropped to one knee. The magician then took a large chiffon cloth, dropped it over his assistant's body—and *immediately* whipped it away to reveal a full-grown Bengal tiger! It was astonishing! I have no idea how he did it, but of this much I'm certain: It was not a miracle. It was a trick.

When Jesus called Lazarus from the tomb—after Lazarus had been dead for four days—the Bible says, in short, "Many of the Jews who . . . had seen what Jesus did, believed in him" (John 11:45). Many? Only *many* believed? Why not *everybody*? That's the trouble with miracles: they're always suspect.

I had a personal experience with this exact thing. I was out on my back deck, sitting in my Jacuzzi, looking up at the stars. Where Jeanne and I live in the mountains above Ashland, the sky is especially crowded with bright, shiny stars. I had been having a particularly difficult week with my church and I decided to ask God if He even wanted me to be a pastor. I prayed, "Lord, if You want me to stay in the ministry, will You please give me a sign?" Immediately—every bit as quickly at the magician's assistant turned into a tiger—I saw a shooting star streak across the entire width of the black sky and disappear beyond the horizon. I knew instantly that it was a clear and miraculous sign of God's affirmation to me. I was thrilled!

For a while.

Then I got to thinking: *Maybe that was just a coincidence. Maybe that was just lucky timing.* So I decided to test God again, and I prayed, "Lord, if that *really* was Your sign to me, please send me another shooting star right now." Of course, there was no second shooting star. But I knew in my heart there was not going to be. I had not even finished my second prayer before I realized I was just as apt to dismiss the second shooting star as I had the first. In fact, I already knew it didn't matter how many shooting stars God sent my way; I would dismiss them all as *coincidence* and continue to have my doubts.

This is why the Bible tells us, "Without faith it is impossible to please God" (Hebrews 11:6). And this is why Paul reminds us, "We walk by faith, not by sight" (2 Corinthians 5:7 NKJV). When Jesus calmed

the storm on the Sea of Galilee, the disciples continued to "fear exceedingly"—even though they had seen
Him perform many miracles—which brings me to the
conclusion of the matter.

Patience is a product of faith. And "faith comes by
hearing, and hearing by the word of God" (Romans
10:17 NKJV). Although the Bible also tells us that we've
each been given a "measure of faith" (Romans 12:3
NKJV), faith is a *learned* strength. It comes with time.
It grows with experience. It increases with observation. It expands through reinforcement. As I've grown
older in the Lord, my faith has grown with me. Here's
why: "They came to the other side of the sea, to the
country of the Gadarenes" (Mark 5:1 NKJV).

I am now sixty-seven years old. As I look back over
my life, I see one recurring and undeniable miracle:
Jesus has always gotten me to the other side of the
storm. This gives me patience when my ship is sinking. This gives me patience when the winds are howl-
ing. This gives me patience when I cannot see land.
This gives me patience when I fear I might drown.
This gives me patience when I start to think that Jesus
is asleep and doesn't care if I perish. He always gets me
to the other side. He always has and He always will.

By the way, the young pastor I talked to fifteen
years ago about the lack of growth in his church took
God's advice and gave his ministry five years to flour-
ish. He's still there.

STEP ONE:
WORK HARD

STEP TWO:
GO IN THE STRENGTH
YOU HAVE

STEP THREE:
FINISH WHAT YOU START

STEP FOUR:
BE PATIENT

HELP OTHER PEOPLE
ALONG THE WAY

*The only ones among you who will be happy are those
who will have sought and found how to serve.*

DR. ALBERT SCHWEITZER

The train pulled into the station, and a tall
gentleman with a bushy mustache and a crop
of thick, white hair emerged from the last car. He
looked around, smiled, and stepped down onto the
wooden platform. From every direction flashbulbs
suddenly ignited like fireflies. Frantic reporters yelled
and waved—writing tablets in hand—wildly trying to
catch his attention. Other folks from all walks of life
gathered on the platform to greet him. Several mothers quickly stooped over to explain to their bewildered
children who this man was, while other mothers nervously gathered their children against them to protect
their little ones from the sudden mayhem.

The city was Chicago. The year was 1953. The man
on the platform was Dr. Albert Schweitzer, medical

missionary to Africa and recent recipient of the 1952 Nobel Peace Prize. The commotion eased a bit, but the reporters continued to call out questions to Schweitzer, hoping to be heard above the din of their colleagues. Other people just smiled, waved, and shouted, "God bless you, Dr. Schweitzer! God bless you!"

City officials and other dignitaries who had managed to hold their place at the front of the crowd now stood before Schweitzer with beaming smiles and outstretched hands. Schweitzer briefly acknowledged their welcome, shook a few hands, but seemed oddly distracted as he looked up and past them to something going on at the far end of the platform. "Excuse me just a moment, won't you?" he asked them suddenly.

Schweitzer then weaved his way through the confused and watchful crowd to where an elderly black woman was struggling with two large suitcases that she was trying to carry to a nearby bus. When Schweitzer got to her, he smiled at her, whispered something to her, and proceeded to carry her suitcases to the bus and load them on for her. He then helped her onto the bus and wished her a safe journey.

The crowd, which had followed him to where the woman was, now was silent. Schweitzer turned back and said, "Sorry to have kept you waiting," and resumed answering questions.

At this point, one of the members of the reception committee leaned over and whispered to a nearby reporter, "That's the first time I ever saw a sermon walking."

NO THERE THERE

Because of my success in the children's book industry, I'm often asked to be a motivational speaker at company luncheons, dinners, retreats, and the like. Whenever I address an adult gathering these days, I invariably move into the final phase of my talk with this brief comment: "Years ago, author and poet Gertrude Stein said, 'When you finally get there, you find that there is no there there.'" That's not exactly what she said. She was referring to returning to her hometown of Oakland, California, after thirty years in Paris, and finding that the city had changed immeasurably. Not finding her childhood home or school where she expected them to be, she said, "What was the use of my having come from Oakland. . . . there is no there there."[11] Today, we most often hear this quote used the way I use it: to sum up the difficulty of trying to find the pot of gold at the end of the rainbow; that is, "When you finally get there, you find that there is no there there." In my seminars and motivational assemblies, that's the moment when the roomful of business hopefuls goes completely silent. People look around at one another, then look at me, and then start nodding in resigned agreement. Everybody gets it. Everybody understands. There is no there there.

Put another way, there's no end point to ambition. There's no final, crowning achievement. There's no grateful sigh of relief from having reached a long-awaited destination. Perhaps that's why Ross Perot said something to the effect of, "The unhappiest people you will ever know are the ones down at the harbor inspecting the nicks and chips on their yachts."

I had to learn this lesson for myself.

The year was 1992. I had just spent several days gathering all my past royalty statements and running totals to see how many children's books I had sold in my career. When I was done, I discovered I had sold more than one million books. It was a major milestone for me, and I was thrilled. My celebration, however, lasted only one day. More quickly than I could have imagined, a deep depression gripped my heart. *Is that all there is?* I asked myself. I could not believe I felt virtually no satisfaction from my accomplishment. Quite the contrary, I had never felt emptier. I had finally come to the same sad conclusion that so many people reach. It was a day that changed my life forever. On a long walk with my wife, Jeanne, and our German shepherd, Duke, I slowly realized that I would never be famous enough, rich enough, popular enough, or *anything* enough to be happy. There was no there there—and there never would be.

Thus began a spiritual journey for both Jeanne and me. My depression had taken a weighty toll on our marriage, and our life together was quickly falling apart. We started going to marriage counseling. We started reading lots of books about how to improve our marriage. We soon noticed that one principle kept surfacing over and over—everywhere we looked: We had a "spiritual hole" in our marriage.

As a result of this nagging insight, we began visiting various churches in our community. Jeanne had been raised Catholic, so we started there. And we rather enjoyed it. I remember feeling particularly holy when the offering plate came around and I sanctimoniously dropped in three one-dollar bills: one for the Father, one for the Son, and one for the Holy Ghost. Believe it or not, this is true, and we still laugh about it. I had been raised as a "sort of" Christian Scientist. I say "sort of" because my parents were the "dump-and-run" type of Christian Scientists, who would drop my brothers and me off for Sunday school, but never actually go inside themselves. In fact, I remember one night when a Christian Science practitioner visited our home and noticed that my parents drank alcohol and smoked cigarettes—a real no-no in Christian Science doctrine. She delicately mentioned this to them, but her words fell on deaf ears. After this, I don't think we had to go to Sunday school anymore.

In any case, Jeanne and I tried Christian Science too, but frankly we couldn't find what we were searching for.

At this point, some friends of ours invited us to their church, Applegate Christian Fellowship in Ruch, Oregon. Ruch is a tiny, unincorporated area in the middle of nowhere, yet Applegate Christian Fellowship had about five thousand people pouring into its parking lot every Sunday. I will never forget the first time I sat in their outdoor sanctuary and took in the view. There were two things I immediately noticed: these Christians looked almost normal, and these Christians knew how to play guitar. For some reason, this latter observation surprised me.

Before I go any further, I need to explain something. I had spent most of my life as an anti-Christian. Not only was I *not* one of them, but I couldn't stand them. Frankly, Christians gave me the willies. Of course, I had based virtually all of my personal theology on one movie, the 1960 blockbuster *Inherit the Wind*, which told the story of Tennessee's famous Scopes Monkey Trial, in which high school biology teacher John Scopes was accused of violating the Butler Act by teaching evolution. My favorite part of the movie was when the clever and fair-minded Henry Drummond makes mincemeat out of goofy old zealot Matthew Harrison Brady. The movie's high spot comes when Drummond goes to work on Brady by challenging him to a duel, using—you got it—the Bible!

Drummond turns to the section in the book of Joshua where the Lord makes the sun stand still in the sky (see Joshua 10:13). He then asks Brady if he thinks this really happened. Brady informs Drummond that he does not question the miracles of the Lord. Drummond nods in mock thoughtfulness, then moves forward. He points out to Brady that if the sun "stopped" in the sky, then the people must have believed that the sun revolved around the earth. Brady simply responds, "The sun stopped." So

Drummond moves in for the kill. He says, "If what you say really happened—if Joshua halted the sun in the sky—that means the earth stopped spinning on its axis; continents toppled over each other, mountains flew into outer space; and the earth, arrested in its orbit, shriveled to a cinder and crashed into the sun." He pauses and says, "How come they missed this bit of news?"

Brady answers, "They missed it because it didn't happen."[12]

Of course, in the movie theater you could not hear Brady's response because my buddies and I were cheering at the tops of our lungs and clapping like thunder for the reasonable and sane argument.

From this point on, I was a firm agnostic. I say "firm" because I *firmly* believed that the only intelligent position a person could take on theology was that nobody could possibly know *for sure* whether there was—or was not—a God. This meant that even the atheists were wrong. I was smugly satisfied with this decision.

So, here I was at Applegate, sitting with five thousand goofy Christians in an outdoor amphitheater, getting ready to hear a sermon about something I already knew was nonsense and did not believe in. And I was right. The sermon was nonsense.

I went back a week later because of how well the Christians played their guitars—and because my wife made me.

Since then, I have often told people, "I went for the

music, but I stayed for the Word." This is mostly true. After a while, I started being able to *hear* what the pastor was saying, and a lot of it made sense. But my true conversion to Christianity did not happen until nearly a year later.

It was November 4, 1993. I had been invited to speak at the California Reading Association's yearly conference, which that year was being held at the convention center in downtown Fresno. It was early evening, about seven o'clock, and I was in my hotel room, reading my Bible and dragging my way through the book of Lamentations. I was doing this—reading my Bible, that is—for two reasons: First, because Jeanne had bought me a new Bible and was smart enough to make it irresistible to me by having my very own name imprinted in gold letters on the cover; Second, because—in deference to Jeanne's desire to see me change—I had agreed to read through the entire book, front to back, and decide for myself whether or not it was true. I felt that, since I was a fairly intelligent person, this approach would certainly tell me whether or not the Bible could be believed. But Lamentations? As mobsters like to say, "fuhgeddaboudit." I was relieved, even elated, when the phone rang. It was Jeanne. We talked for a couple of minutes about the conference—about my presentations, my book sales, and so forth—but then she cut to the chase. "How is your Bible reading coming?"

I threw myself on the mercy of the court. "Terrible," I whined. "I am reading Lamentations and I am ready to give up!"

Jeanne never missed a beat. "Skip ahead to John," she said.

Whenever I tell this story, I like to mention that I am *not* a skip-ahead kind of guy. I am very precise. I am very organized. I am laboriously methodical. I do not skip ahead—ever. It is one of my strengths. On the other hand, I *was* reading Lamentations. So I skipped ahead to the gospel of John.

Then everything happened at once.

I read: "In the beginning was the Word, and the Word was with God, and the Word was God" (John 1:1 KJV). The first thing that struck me was that this made no sense. The second thing that struck me was that there was no hidden agenda in this sentence: John was not trying to convince me to "vote for Pedro," so to speak. It was quite the contrary. This man was not trying to convince me to *do* anything. He was carefully, and unemotionally, explaining some vast concept to me. I liked that. Then I read: "He was in the world, and the world was made by him, and the world knew him not" (John 1:10 KJV). Something in this verse rang true. The words stirred a memory deep within me about an old spiritual, *Sweet Little Jesus Boy*, with the recurring lyric, "We didn't know who You wuz." I mulled this over: *The world knew Him not / We didn't know who You wuz.* It was as if bits and pieces of a long lost memory—thoughts that once belonged to me, thoughts that never should have fallen into the darkness—were now quickly reassembling themselves in my brain, forming something ancient and fundamental. Then I reached verse 14 and read, "And the Word was made flesh, and dwelt among us," and that did it.

What I'm about to say will sound heretical to some, but it is the Lord's own truth about what happened next. This verse jarred yet another memory of mine about an old 3-D science-fiction movie I saw back in the 1950s. The story was about some benevolent alien creatures that land their tiny spaceship on earth, only to find that earthlings are terrified by their appearance. To resolve this, one alien fakes a humanoid countenance and begins communicating with the earthlings. Doing better than he ever expected—or set out to do—he captures the heart of a beautiful news reporter, and they eventually start cooing and cuddling and nuzzling. The big moment comes when the reporter, suddenly sensing the truth about her handsome alien, pleads with him to reveal his true form to her. He warns, "You could not bear to look at me as I am." She says, "Oh, let's have a look-see anyway." When the creature finally relents and reveals himself to her, the reporter screams because she realizes she has been kissing an eight-foot-tall lobster.

I'm glad God meets us where we are—or I would never have been allowed into the kingdom. He took this memory of mine about the disguised alien and applied it to Himself. In other words, God came to earth in the only form we could accept: as one of us. Also—like the alien in my 3-D epic—God knew that we could not bear to look at Him as He really is. In the book of Exodus, Moses asks God to show him His glory. But the Lord answers, "I will cause all my goodness to pass in front of you, and I will proclaim my name, the LORD, in your presence.... But ... you cannot see my face, for no one may see me and live" (Exodus 33:18–20).

In any case, I sat there alone, in the semidarkness of my little hotel room, and whispered aloud to myself, "Is it possible all this stuff is true?"

Then I went to bed.

The following morning, I got into my car and drove about fifty miles west on Highway 152 to a little town called Los Banos. I was scheduled to do four days of school visits there, with the usual book signings and book selling. I arrived earlier than I had expected, so I checked into my motel and then went for a walk.

Many born-again Christians cannot pinpoint the exact moment when their conversion experience happened to them. My wife, Jeanne, is one of these. She does not remember any particular event that signaled the beginning of her faith in Christ. Her conversion was slow-rolling and subtle. One day, she just knew that Jesus Christ was her Lord and Savior. This was not true for me. I was walking along a well-worn dirt path that paralleled the main thoroughfare of Los Banos and gazing absently through a chain-link fence that surrounded a local elementary school. Suddenly, I stopped dead in my tracks. With my heart in my throat, I looked up at the sky and nervously asked, "Jesus, are You real?" In the next moment, cold sweat broke out across my back and began trickling down my spine. I started shaking all over. He was real.

RUNNING ON EMPTY

Obviously, I'm not the only person to notice that the principle of "there is no there there" applies perfectly to why so many careers, and lives, come up empty. A few years back, I was invited to speak at an elementary school in Fort Lauderdale, Florida. After I had given my presentations, I was taken to a local church, Calvary Chapel of Fort Lauderdale, for dinner. This may seem like an odd choice—and location—for a restaurant, but several of the staff at the elementary school knew I was a pastor and that this fellowship had evolved from the same mother church as mine: Pastor Chuck Smith's Calvary Chapel of Costa Mesa. So we went there and dined.

There is almost no way to describe the size of Calvary Chapel of Fort Lauderdale. The attendance exceeds 22,000 people each and every Sunday, and the facility looks more like a college campus than a church. I remember walking for what seemed like two and a half miles before we got to the sanctuary—and then seeing a teensy weensy photograph of the pastor, Bob Coy, on the wall opposite the large room. The contrast between the huge church and the tiny photograph reminded me of Psalm 127:1: "Unless the LORD builds the house, the builders labor in vain."

Only God could have done this, I thought to myself. In 1958, missionary Elisabeth Elliot sat in her hut in the jungles of Ecuador and quietly watched once-fierce Auca Indians sharing the compound with her children. These were the same Aucas who, two years earlier, had killed her husband, Jim, and five coworkers, along the Curaray River, using wooden spears. They now belonged to Christ. Elisabeth Elliot writes: "How did this come to be? Only God, who made iron swim, who caused the sun to stand still, in whose hand is the breath of every living thing—only *this* God, who is *our* God forever and ever, could have done it."[13] Amen, Sister Elisabeth. This was exactly how I felt about the colossal size of Calvary Chapel in Fort Lauderdale. Only *this* God, who is *our* God, could have done it.

And yes, Bob Coy's church was *so big* that they even had their own restaurant. I guess that's because a person could starve to death just walking from the Sunday school to the sanctuary.

Pastor Bob Coy is a remarkable person. He is hysterically funny, but also deeply grounded in his faith. A newspaper reporter who sat in on one of his services described him as a cross between Billy Graham and Billy Crystal. Though Pastor Bob doesn't remember me, I met him once at a pastors' retreat on the South Shore of Lake Tahoe. He gave a hilarious teaching about Aaron and Hur holding up Moses' arms at the Battle of Rephidim—and getting so bored with the job that they start grooming their fingernails and sending out for Diet Cokes. Joshua, in the meantime, was valiantly sword-fighting the entire Amalekite army in the valley below. Coy's point was that Aaron and Hur are always credited with being the types of "undergirders" all pastors need, when, in fact, Joshua was doing the real work. We laughed so hard we could barely breathe. Being the encourager that I am, I quickly sought out Bob Coy to thank him for being such a blessing to all of us. He warmly thanked me and turned his attention to the multitude of other pastors who had also come to thank him.

The next morning at breakfast, however, he sheepishly shared his wife's response to his talk the night before. She had gotten on his case, thinking he'd gone too far.

What I remember most about Bob Coy, though, is the personal testimony he gave to his church about fifteen years ago. It was both fascinating and inspiring. It has since been published in book form as *One Surrendered Life*.

Bob was working in the music industry in Las Vegas. His main job was to drive celebrity rock groups around Vegas in a limousine and provide them with whatever they wanted—which he did. He noted, though, that virtually all of these rock stars were miserably unhappy people. He said, "As I listened to them whining and complaining in the backseat, I started asking myself, 'If these guys have everything in the world that anybody is supposed to want—money, drugs, girls, fame—and they still aren't happy, then who is?'"

That's a good question. This observation eventually changed his life.

To a degree, fame and fortune are always deceptive

illusions. They solve nothing. That's exactly what Bob Coy witnessed. And that's exactly what I learned that day when I counted up all my book sales: All the success in the world cannot fill the empty spot inside us that is crying out for God.

HAPPINESS

There's an old story about a man who is determined to discover the meaning of life. He sells everything he has in order to travel the globe looking for answers. After much searching, he finally hears about a wise, old sage, living in a cave somewhere in the Himalayas, who has the answer he has been looking for. The traveler then makes an arduous four-day climb, struggling up one sheer cliff after another, until he finally arrives at the entrance to the old man's cave. He steps inside and finds the wise man sitting on the floor, deep in meditation. Finally the old man looks up and asks, "What is it you want, my son?"

The traveler answers, "I have given up everything I have—my money, my job, my possessions, even my family—to come here to ask you just one question."

"Yes, my son?" the old man says.

The traveler draws a deep breath and asks, "Sir, what is the meaning of life?"

The wise man nods slowly, smiles benevolently, and says, "My son, life is a fountain." Then he lowers his head again.

The traveler now stands in complete silence, studying the old man's face. Then, after about five *very long* seconds, he explodes in frustration. "Let me get this straight: I gave up everything I had, I spent every cent I made, I left my family and friends and traveled the entire world for years—just to have you tell me is that 'life is a fountain'?"

At this point, the wise man looks up again, draws a sharp bead on the traveler, and says, "You mean it's not?"

Oh, well. That story was very funny in high school.

Invariably, when people are searching for "the meaning of life," what they're really searching for is some kind of satisfaction, contentment, fulfillment, or happiness for all their efforts. But usually they look to their *possessions* to give them this. This rarely works.

On the night of the Last Supper, when everyone had finished eating, Jesus girded Himself with a towel and began washing the disciples' feet. He moved around the whole room—performing a task normally reserved for the lowest of the slaves—and when He had finished He sat down again. He said, "Now that I, your Lord and Teacher, have washed your feet, you also should wash one another's feet. I have set you an example that you should do as I have done for you." Then He added, "Now that you know these things, you will be blessed if you do them" (John 13:14-15, 17). The Greek word that Jesus uses for "blessed" is *makarios*, which means both *happy* and *blessed*. So Jesus is telling His disciples that, if they will serve one another, they will be happy and blessed. Jesus also tells His disciples that it is not enough just to "know" these things or "understand" these things, but they must *do* these things. There's the rub. Christ's brother James puts it this way: "Faith without works is dead" (James 2:20 NKJV). Mahatma Gandhi expressed a similar sentiment: "To give pleasure to a single heart by a single act is better than a thousand heads bowed in prayer." I could not agree more.

Wherever I go, whenever I speak to any gathering of people, young or old, I always tell them that one of the most important things I have learned in my entire life is this: "It is not what I take in that fills me; it is what I give out." I say this about four times just to let it sink in, and people seem to understand. Also, I preach this from the pulpit, because Christians also need to be reminded that "giving out" is what fills us.

Each year, in our little town of Ashland, a local Christian fellowship holds a free community-wide Christmas dinner, focusing primarily on feeding the poor and the homeless. I first got involved in this event back in 1996 when Andy Green, the former pastor of our church, invited me to bring my guitar and sing a few Christmas carols to the long line of folks standing outside in the cold, patiently waiting to enter the food kitchen. I happily agreed, and that Christmas morning, Jeanne and I both showed up ready to help: I played my guitar and sang Christmas carols, and she worked in the food line, happily serving healthful scoops of hot food to all who attended—which turned out to be in excess of one thousand people.

Although Jeanne and I both had been scheduled to work only one, concurrent two-hour shift, we ended up staying all day. What Jesus said to His disciples after washing their feet was, of course, right on the mark: Jeanne and I drove home seven hours later feeling spiritually stuffed beyond anything we had ever experience or imagined—even beyond our capacity! To put it mildly, we were *makarios*! We were extraordinarily *happy* and *blessed*! We have continued to take part in this event ever since. And we are always *makarios*.

This is what happens when we are willing to serve others.

The event had such an impact on me that I eventually sat down and wrote the children's book called *Heartprints*. The definition of the word *heartprint* is at the bottom of the front cover of the book. It reads: "Heartprint: the impression left behind by a deliberate act of kindness." The defining text, however, is this:

> A heartprint is formed
> When we do something kind.
> Our love touches others,
> Leaving heartprints behind.

My encouragement to you is to touch as many lives with love—with heartprints—as you possibly can. It's so easy, too! It is a kind word to the checker at the grocery store. It is a friendly hello to the mailman. It is a moment of listening to the lonely neighbor. It is a simple "thank-you" to the waiter who serves your food. Leaving a heartprint simply means momentarily—and intentionally—brightening someone else's day.

My favorite verse in the book is this:

> Yes, each little kindness
> Leaves heartprints that say,
> "A very nice person
> Has been here today."

I like that. Something has been left behind. Something is still resonating in the air. The room is still bright. Spirits are still high. Something very nice has just happened. Someone very nice has just passed by. *Can you feel it? Can you feel it, too?*

A good friend of mine, a fellow pastor, once said to me, "Your book kind of reminds me of Psalm 23:6 (NKJV), where the psalmist says, 'Surely goodness and mercy shall follow me all the days of my life.'" I agree. This is exactly what my book is about. At some point in our lives, we need to ask ourselves, "What am I leaving behind? What blessings are floating in my wake? Are goodness and mercy following me? Are people better off because I passed by? Am I helping others along the way? Am I making a difference? Does my life *matter*?"

DEAD MEN WALKING

I keep seeing the same homeless man walking around Ashland. He is fairly young, in his thirties I would guess, but time and his lifestyle have taken their toll on his appearance and on his mind. His skin is permanently sun darkened, his clothes are ragged and sooty, and his hair is a mixture of shaved spots and wild black tresses. Playing with matches recently, he burned down half a neighborhood near our local golf course. Yet, almost everyone—including me and the judicial system—seems to have a sympathetic heart for him.

What I have observed most about this unfortunate young man is that he never stops walking around. He walks all over the town of Ashland. He walks on every street. He walks on every sidewalk. He walks on every footpath. Day after day, month after month, year after year, he just keeps walking around. I remember watching him one day and thinking to myself, *How does he do it? How does he just keep walking around all the time?* Then it struck me. If it were not for the fact that I have eternal life—and that the work I am doing for the Lord has eternal consequences—there would be no difference between him and me. I would be just one more person walking around on this planet.

It was a Wednesday evening at Applegate Christian Fellowship, and about three hundred of us were sitting in the sanctuary—Bibles on our laps, pencils in our hands—taking notes as Pastor Jon Courson taught us the midweek Bible study. Jon is a very powerfully built individual. He has been lifting weights faithfully since high school, and it shows. He has large shoulders, a muscular back, and big biceps. And much to his credit, he has not sculpted his body to look like

Adonis. He is just plain *big*. Besides the discovery that Christians could play guitars, Jon's powerful build also intrigued me. Every minister I had ever known looked like Pinky Lee—a rail-thin 1950s children's TV star. But Jon looked more like The Hulk. Before that, I didn't know that *any* Christians lifted weights.

I don't remember what Jon was teaching that evening, but I do remember watching him banter with the audience—and then suddenly, it was as if I had been hit by spiritual lightning as a thought came crashing into my brain. In that moment, I knew that what Jon was doing, sharing the Bible, was exactly what I had been looking for my whole life! That's why I was there. That's why I was sitting in *that* sanctuary on *that* particular evening. Here was a person who was performing exactly the kind of work I needed to be performing. Here was a guy whose work actually meant something. Here was a guy with *a life that mattered!* I decided right then and there to go into the ministry. All I needed to do was find out how.

Divine appointments are wonderful. They seem to happen when you need them most and expect them least. And they are always recognizable looking back.

The following Tuesday afternoon, I ran into one of Jon Courson's assistant pastors at a local shopping mall. I didn't waste any time with formalities, I just flatly asked him, "How do I get into the ministry?"

His answer sounded like a put-off. He said, "Just hang around after Sunday service and pray with people." I doubted that would ever amount to anything, but I did what he suggested, and odd things started to happen—right away.

A few weeks later, I was sitting on a bench outside the dining area of Applegate's Mountain Top Retreat Center, and suddenly Jon Courson plopped down next to me. He said, "P.K., how would you feel about starting a men's morning Bible study?"

Without having a single clue what this activity might entail, I answered, "Sure, I would love to." This led to a weekly Tuesday morning Bible study that I led for the next year and a half.

Sometime during the months that followed, an assistant pastor at Applegate, one who had been called to plant a church in the mountains above Ashland in the community of Green Springs, asked me if I would like to help him with this ministry. Again, not having a clue what this would entail, I said, "Sure, I would love to."

Eight months later, he was asked to become the pastor of a sister fellowship in the Salem area. He took the job. Then he and the congregation asked me if I would be the new pastor in Green Springs. I said, "Sure, I would love to."

That was July 1995. I have been serving God as a pastor ever since—walking around, but now with purpose.

LITTLE THINGS MEAN A LOT

On that best portion of a good man's life,
His little, nameless, unremembered, acts
Of kindness and of love.

—William Wordsworth[14]

There are many ways to live a life that matters and many ways to make a difference with the time and skills we've been given.

Not long ago, I attended a meeting of Ashland's local Rotary Club. One of the traditions of Rotary is to use a fellow Rotarian as the meeting's sergeant-at-arms and to have him levy "fines" on people for just about anything he can think of. Someone might be fined because they just bought a new car or a new home. Someone might be fined simply because they had the bad luck to appear on TV or in the newspaper. All of these so-called fines are just an enjoyable way to raise donations for the various Rotary charities.

At this particular meeting, the sergeant-at-arms posed this question: "What inscription would you like to see on your headstone?"

I'm not sure how he intended to grade the answers—and I don't even remember what anybody said—but I have never forgotten my own response to this question. Though I had never considered this before in my life, I knew immediately—and exactly—what I wanted inscribed on my tombstone:

> Here lies P.K. Hallinan.
> People were happy to see him.

Of course, I knew some vandal would come along later and add the word *go* at the end. But all in all, I thought it was a nice sentiment.

I pondered this answer quite a bit over the next few

days, and I soon added it to my motivational speeches, seminars, and school assemblies. After sharing my story about the Rotary Club meeting, I look around the room at my audience and ask, "So—are people happy to see you? Do people light up when you enter the room? Are people visibly glad that you have arrived?—and if not, how come?" It always hits a nerve with *someone.* So let me ask you, dear reader, the same question:

Are people happy to see you? And if not, how come?

I like how Mother Teresa put this same idea. She said, "Let no one ever come to you without coming away better and happier." More words to live by.

For years I argued with the Wizard of Oz when he would tell the Tin Man, "Remember, my friend, a heart is not measured by how much you love but by how much you are loved by others." One day, I finally understood what he meant. He meant that it is easy to *say* that you love people. It is easy to *say* that you are a loving person. But if nobody loves you back, then in the words of Ricky Ricardo, "Lucy, you got some 'splaining to do!" Why don't people love you? Why aren't people happy to see you? The answer? It may be that you don't know what love actually is.

By the way, the sergeant-at-arms did not call on me that day, and I was not fined.

LOVING OUR NEIGHBOR

> Behold, a certain lawyer stood up and tested Him, saying, "Teacher, what shall I do to inherit eternal life?" (Luke 10:25 NKJV)

You may recognize this verse of Scripture as the beginning of the story of the Good Samaritan. A student of Jewish Law stands up and asks Jesus a question that he hopes will force Jesus to say something that can be interpreted as blasphemous; something the Pharisees can use to arrest Jesus—at last. The lawyer asks, "How can I have eternal life?" He is not referring to eternal life as you and I understand it but to what was known at that time, in that culture, as the "full-orbed" life, meaning the most blessed and prosperous life now—and on into eternity.

Jesus responds by asking the lawyer what the Law says. The lawyer responds—putting it briefly—"Love God and love your neighbor." Jesus congratulates him on his answer, and then adds, "*Do* this and you will live" (Luke 10:28, emphasis added). But the lawyer feels embarrassed and stammers, "And who is my neighbor?" (v. 29).

Over the years, I tended to scoff at this question from the lawyer as self-defensive and self-serving. But I have since changed my mind. It is actually a very good question. Today we might ask, "Yes, but what if my neighbor is a drunk? What if my neighbor is a lout? What if my neighbor blasts his stereo night and day? What if my neighbor is an ex-con?" Or more generically, "What if my neighbor is not lovable? What then?"

Jesus answers the man's question by telling the story of a traveler who is beaten, robbed, and left for dead by thieves on the road to Jericho. A priest passes him by. A Levite passes him by. But a Samaritan—a man from a culture despised by the Jews—stops and helps the victim. Jesus then asks the lawyer, "Which of these three do you think was a neighbor to the man who fell into the hands of robbers?" The lawyer cannot even bear to say the word *Samaritan*, so he answers, "The one who had mercy on him." Jesus responds, "Go and do likewise" (vv. 36–37).

There are many things about these verses that I like. The first is that Jesus takes the lawyer's question, "Who is my neighbor?" and converts it into a different, more important question: "Who is *a* neighbor?" The second thing I like is that this Scripture has a powerful emphasis on the word *do*. The lawyer asks, "What must I *do*?" Jesus responds, "*Do* this and you will live." Then later, "Go, and *do* likewise." I find a theme here. *Do*ing for my neighbor is the key to *loving* my neighbor.

I also like the lawyer's response to Jesus' question about which passerby acted like a neighbor to the victim. The lawyer answers: "The one who had mercy on him." This is exactly correct and confirms my *"doing"* theory of what love really is. Let us note that the lawyer did not say, "He that *felt* mercy."

You see, the priest might have *felt* mercy, but how can we know? The Levite might have *felt* mercy, but how can we know? Since neither of these two people ever *showed* mercy, we will never know what they were *feeling*. And that's the point.

This section of Scripture is given to us specifically

so that we will understand the importance of—and the value of—*do*ing the Lord's work. Christ's brother James puts it this way: "Be doers of the word, and not hearers only, deceiving yourselves" (James 1:22 NKJV). I say, "Amen" to this. If I want to have a *full-orbed* life; if I want to have the most blessed and prosperous life now, and on into eternity; if I want to enjoy the fruits of the kingdom life to their fullest, I need to be someone who *shows* mercy—not just *feels* mercy—no matter who my neighbor is.

Jesus said to the lawyer, "Do this and you will live." But to those of us who already have eternal life in Him, Jesus says, "Live, and do this." In other words, as Christians we are not *do*ing in order to *get* something from God; we are *do*ing in order to *give* something to God. Which is? When we love our neighbors as ourselves—when we *show* mercy and not just *feel* it—we are giving God a face in the world. We are giving God a smile. We are giving God friendly eyes. We are giving God warm laughter. We are giving God a body so He can once again walk among us. We are showing the world who God is—a God of infinite grace and infinite mercy, who loves us so much that He died for us.

Yes, but suppose I can't stand my neighbor? Love him anyway. Yes, but what if he's a drunk? Love him anyway. Yes, but what if he's foul-mouthed and cruel? Love him anyway. Yes, but how can I make myself feel love for someone I despise? You can't—love him anyway.

You see, love is not a feeling. Love is a *doing*.

Let me say that again so you don't miss it: Love is not a feeling. Love is a *doing*. Love, in God's realm, is a *decision* to act lovingly toward people, regardless of how we may *feel* about them. Besides, we are not asked to offer people *our* love—which is finite and changeable. We are asked to offer them *God's* love—which is infinite and changeless. In this sense, love should never be limited by its object (others); its extent and quality are under the control of its subject (us). Of course, it's also nice to know that, usually, "form follows function." This means that if I am bound and determined to love someone I don't even like—long enough and demonstrably enough—in time, I usually will find myself actually *feeling* love for this person.

Deciding to love people—deciding to help other people along the way—is the best decision that you will ever make. As we move forward with our determination to serve God by loving others, it is comforting to remember this: "All things are possible with God" (Mark 10:27).

In this sense, there is a there there, after all.

One final note: Jesus never asks us to do anything that He Himself has not already done. He loved the unlovable. He embraced the outcasts. He cleansed the unclean. He fed the hungry. He healed the sick. He forgave the sinners. He helped anyone the Father put in His path. We need to do this, too. The term *Christian* means "little Christ." We are now standing where Jesus once stood. We are now doing what Jesus once did. We are now helping the Father finish His work—"the saving of many lives" (Genesis 50:20).

"Now that you know these things, you will be blessed if you do them" (John 13:17).

STEP ONE:
WORK HARD

STEP TWO:
GO IN THE STRENGTH
YOU HAVE

STEP THREE:
FINISH WHAT YOU START

STEP FOUR:
BE PATIENT

STEP FIVE:
HELP OTHER PEOPLE
ALONG HE WAY

Conclusion

Would it have been worth while
If one, settling a pillow or throwing off a shawl,
And turning toward the window, should say:
"That is not it at all,
That is not what I meant, at all."

T. S. Eliot, "The Love Song of
J. Alfred Prufrock"

One of the worst feelings I can imagine is getting to the end of my life and realizing I had never expressed who I was—that my life did not demonstrate what I believed or how I felt. To put it more succinctly: that my life did not matter.

How empty I would feel—how utterly ashamed I would be—to stand before God and say, "That is not it at all. That is not what I meant, at all."

In Charles Dickens's *A Christmas Carol*, Ebenezer Scrooge is visited in his bed chamber by the ghost of his old business partner, Jacob Marley. Marley's ghost is wearing an iron chain and wailing loudly as he bemoans his past mistakes. "No space of regret can make amends for one life's opportunities misused!" he sobs. "Yet such was I! Oh! Such was I!"

At this point, the terrified Scrooge applies Marley's words to himself. He stammers, "But you were always a good man of business, Jacob."

"Business!" Marley shrieks. "Mankind was my business!"[15] He added that people, not business, should have been the focus of his life, a life that then would have been characterized by charity, mercy, forbearance, and benevolence.

As I mentioned in Step Two, there are no new ideas, only new treatments. This conversation between Scrooge and Marley was written in 1843, yet it is as accurate and meaningful today as it was then. Mankind is our business.

Many people want to help others, but they don't know where, or how, to start. Here's where: Start where you are. Here's how: Start with a smile.

Each morning as I go for my daily jog around the city of Ashland, I often take a short detour along a dirt path that passes through the local cemetery. Whenever I do this, I am faithful to read a headstone that caught my eye several years ago. It is in the southeast corner of the little cemetery, and it reads:

Almira A. Starr
Born: Nov. 25, 1864
Went to sleep in the Lord: Oct. 12, 1920
Mark 14:8 She hath done what she could.

She hath done what she could. What a great legacy. Here is the context of this verse: Jesus is in the town of Bethany, just five miles outside of Jerusalem, at the home of Simon the Leper. A woman, presumably Mary (Martha's sister) comes in with a jar of very expensive perfume and uses the perfume to anoint Jesus' head. The disciples are taken aback and rebuke her for her wastefulness. They say: "Why this waste of perfume? It could have been sold for more than a year's wages, and the money given to the poor." But Jesus quickly waves them off. "Leave her alone," He says. "She has done a beautiful thing to me." He tells them that the poor will always be with them, but that He is departing soon. "She did what she could," He says. "She poured perfume on my body beforehand to prepare for my burial." Then He says, "Truly I tell you, wherever the gospel is preached throughout the world, what she has done will also be told, in memory of her" (Mark 14:3-9).

What she has done will be told, in memory of her. This is true for all of us: What we *do* will be told as a memorial to us. Our memorial will be what we have *done* with this precious life God has given us. And I believe that Almira A. Starr did it perfectly. She did what she *could*.

This is all that God asks.

Mankind is our business. This life is not about *getting*. This life is about *giving*. This life is about caring. It is about helping. It is about serving. It is about sharing. It is about loving a child. It is about changing a life. And sometimes, it is about saving a life.

At the end of our lives, these are the things that matter.

In closing, if you are a person who is loving; if you are a person who is giving; if you are a person who is supportive, who is loyal, who leaves heartprints, who leaves people thinking, *A very nice person has been here today* . . . then you have lived a worthwhile and substantial life. You have lived a life that matters.

May goodness and mercy follow you all the days of your life, and may you dwell in the house of the Lord forever.

God bless you.

POSTSCRIPT

If you declare with your mouth, "Jesus is Lord,"
and believe in your heart that God raised him
from the dead, you will be saved.

ROMANS 10:9

Perhaps as you read this book, you felt a longing in your heart. This "longing" is for Jesus Christ. Your heart will always feel empty without Him. But this is very easy to fix. If you would like to fill your emptiness—and be completely sure that you are going to spend eternity with Jesus in heaven—just pray the prayer below, from your heart. Once you have done this, go tell someone about it; a family member, a Christian neighbor, a pastor, or any trusted friend will do. It's just that simple.

Let's pray:

Dear Lord Jesus,
I believe You are the Son of God. I believe You
died for my sins and rose again for my salvation.
I confess I am a sinner. I have done things I am

ashamed of. But I want to turn from my sins. I invite You now to come into my heart, take over my life, and change me into the person You want me to be. And I ask You to take me to heaven when I die. In Your name, I pray, Lord. Amen.

Welcome to the family!

NOTES

1. "Research conducted by *Time* magazine in 2010 indicated that less than half of American workers (45%) are satisfied with their jobs." "Employee Engagement Statistics," Resources for Entrepreneurs website, http://www.gaebler.com/Employee -Engagement-Statistics.htm.

2. Davy Crockett, *A Narrative of the Life of David Crockett, of the State of Tennessee* (Philadelphia: E. L. Carey and A. Hart, 1834), 1.

3. Lao Tzu, *The Way of Life (Dao de jing)*, trans. R. B. Blakney (New York: Penguin, 2001), 117.

4. Corrie ten Boom, *Tramp for the Lord* (New York: Jove, 2008), 176.

5. Malcolm Muggeridge, *Something Beautiful for God* (New York: Harper and Row, 1971), 22.

6. Richard J. Krejcir, "Statistics on Pastors: What Is Going on with the Pastors in America?" Schaeffer Institute, 2007, http://www.intothyword.org /apps/articles/default.asp?articleid=36562&colu mnid=3958.

7. *Papillon*, directed by Franklin J. Schaffner (Hacienda Heights, California: Allied Artists Pictures, 1973), DVD.

8. William E. Hartpole Lecky, *History of European Morals from Augustus to Charlemagne*, vol. 2 (New York: D. Appleton and Co., 1869), 9.

9. *On the Waterfront*, directed by Elia Kazan (Los Angeles: Columbia Pictures, 1954), DVD.

10. Andre Bernard, *Rotten Rejections* (Long Island, New York: Pushcart Press, 1990).

11. Gertrude Stein, *Everybody's Autobiography* (Indiana University: Exact Change, 1933), 298.

12. *Inherit the Wind*, directed by Stanley Kramer (1960; Universal City, CA: Stanley Kramer Productions), DVD. The quotes are my paraphrases of dialogue from the movie.

13. Elisabeth Elliot, *Through Gates of Splendor*, 40th ann. ed. (Wheaton, IL: Tyndale House, 1981), 257.

14. William Wordsworth, "Lines: Written a Few Miles Above Tintern Abbey, On Revisiting the Banks of the Wye during a Tour, July 13, 1798," vol. 1 of *Lyrical Ballads, with Pastoral and other Poems, in Two Volumes*, 3rd ed. (London: T. N. Longman and O. Rees, 1802), 193.

15. Charles Dickens, *A Christmas Carol* (St. Louis: MCE Publishing Co., 1996), 61.

About the Author

P.K. Hallinan is an ordained minister, a children's author/illustrator of more than ninety books, and a nationally noted speaker, whose motivational assembly, Find a Hole and Fill It, has touched thousands of lives.

He lives with his wife, Jeanne, two dogs, and a very annoying cat in the mountains of Oregon.